I0804502

ILLUMINATING MINISTRY

a journal

Volume II

Editors
Victor J. Klimoski
Barbara Sutton

Saint John's
SCHOOL OF THEOLOGY·SEMINARY
Prepare to Serve

www1.csbsju.edu/sot

The images contained in *Illuminating Ministry: A Journal* are reproductions of the illuminations found in *The Saint John's Bible.* A monumental achievement and historic undertaking, *The Saint John's Bible* is the only handwritten and illuminated Bible commissioned by a Benedictine Abbey since the advent of the printing press more than five hundred years ago. In the Middle Ages, monasteries helped preserve knowledge and culture for the sake of the greater community. By commissioning a handwritten Bible, Saint John's Abbey and University in Collegeville, Minnesota, revives a tradition and affirms a commitment to the study of Scripture, to the book arts, and to educational, artistic, and spiritual pursuits. *The Saint John's Bible* is a unique blend of ancient methods, materials, and tools with modern themes, images, and technology. It is being made entirely by hand and uses traditional materials including inks, hand-ground pigments, and gold and silver leaf. The renowned calligrapher and illuminator Donald Jackson, in collaboration with scribes, artists, and theologians, directs the creation of *The Saint John's Bible.* When all seven volumes of *The Saint John's Bible* are completed, they will be carefully preserved at the Hill Museum & Manuscript Library at Saint John's University and will be made available as the focus of educational instruction in many forms. Visit www.saintjohnsbible.org to learn more.

This book was edited by Victor J. Klimoski, Director, Lifelong Learning, and Barbara Sutton, Associate Dean, Formation and Outreach, School of Theology•Seminary, Saint John's University with funding from the Lilly Endowment.

ISBN 978-0-8146-3371-7

CONTENTS

INTRODUCTION

This collection of pastoral stories and reflections illustrate the power of "ordinary theology." Such a form of theology conveys the insight and wisdom that emerges from the life of pastoral leaders alert to how events reveal God's mystery and grace. Being ordinary is not about being simple or uncomplicated but about being attentive to the instruction inherent in daily life.

This journal began with a retreat at Saint John's Abbey Guesthouse with the authors who come from different ministerial vocations. Each chapter in this journal takes as its launch point a charism or value in Benedictine spirituality rooted in St. Benedict's fundamental commitment: that it is the Gospel that shapes, direct, and deepens all efforts to be faithful disciples of Christ. Participants were randomly assigned one of the seven charisms selected for the project and arrived with a story to tell that captured for them what the charism meant. As we discussed each story, the authors discovered its link to an illumination from *The Saint John's Bible*. Meditation on the illumination by the group took the story to a deeper level and enabled the author to probe her or his experience in light of the scriptures and in relationship to the assigned charism.

We believe that the stories of ministry are an important way to illuminate Christian life. They help us pay close attention to how discipleship values find expression in the work and experiences that characterize ministry. They become occasions for connecting what might seem part of an ordinary course of events in life to a broader, deeper narrative that prompts one to sit up straight, with eyes wide open. Like an illumination in *The Saint John's Bible*, the stories weave together the insight these ministers have gained from their practice of ministry with a wisdom that reaches back across generations.

This resource journal supports the practice of theological reflection as an essential habit of excellent ministry. The stories invite exploration and encourage those who read them to retrieve their own stories and to consider the revelation inherent in their work, in their relationships, and in their journeys to be faithful and faith-filled disciples. The authors in this volume share their insights into how the Scriptures—and the illuminations—influence how they as ministers interpret their pastoral experiences. They also provide commentaries on seven charisms of discipleship, showing how each continues as a dynamic force in individual lives and in communities. They model a process of theological transformation that moves a good story to the level of pastoral insight.

This text benefited from the final proofing of Laura Bourke, our summer graduate assistant. We are grateful to the writing team for their commitment to this process. Each brought a unique perspective and rich background so that our conversations became mutually formative. Readers benefit from the wisdom of this group, and the church benefits from their whole-hearted dedication to their vocational callings.

Victor Klimoski
Barbara Sutton
Editors

GROUP SPIRITUAL COMPANIONING

"When we wish to suggest our wants to persons of high station, we do not presume to do so except with humility and reverence. How much the more, then, are complete humility and pure devotion necessary in supplication of the Lord who is God of the universe! And let us be assured that it is not in saying a great deal that we shall be heard (Matt 6:7), but in purity of heart and in tears of compunction." Rule of St. Benedict 20

Most people find it helpful to have someone to companion them on their faith journey as they seek to deepen their relationship with God. Such companionship increases our capacity to listen to God in prayer and through one another as we grow in Christian community and in our sense of God's path for us. Spiritual companioning is a process that focuses on conscious development of the relationship between a person and God in either one-to-one spiritual direction or in small group settings.

Spiritual companioning groups gather to share life experiences, listen to the promptings of God in the stories of others, and explore the call to ministry and the discernment of gifts. At the heart of these gatherings is the opportunity to pray together. Groups also strive to promote an atmosphere of listening and responding to God's voice in daily experiences, enkindling our desires to be more fully alive and active in the world and in service to the church. They also provide an opportunity for each person to receive support and challenge from a small community of peers who are listening to and praying for each other. The members of the group serve as spiritual companions for each other.

This spiritual companioning journal is designed for both personal and communal discernment. In spiritual companioning groups, four to five people within a ninety-minute time frame seem most effective for group process. The prayer movement through this journal is based on *lectio divina.* While there is no standard way to do *lectio*, there are generally seven aspects to this spiritual practice:

- **Illuminating Ministry**: Read the story aloud. Listen with the ear of your heart. Respond to these questions in your journal: In what ways does your own experience connect with this story? How does this story shape your vocational call? Share a response with your group. (25 minutes)
- **Lectio**/Listening: Proclaim the scripture passage. Listen for God's word or a passage that touches the heart. Ruminate on the Word, turning it over in your heart and mind. Share the word aloud. (10 minutes)
- **Meditatio**/Meditating: Ruminate on God's word. Allow the word or passage to dwell within you. Allow this pondering to invite you into dialogue with God. What does the word or phrase you have chosen mean to you today? Share with your group. (15 minutes)
- **Visio**/Seeing: Return to God's word for the purpose of "seeing with the eyes of faith" Christ in the illuminated word. As the scripture is read again, fix your gaze on the illumination. What draws you into this illumination? What do you see? Where do you meet God in this illumination? Ask God to open the eyes of your heart, enabling you to see what God wants you to see. Be open to images, thoughts, impressions and feelings that come into your awareness. Share with your group what you see. Typically one begins with a literal interpretation. Then illuminate its meaning by contextualizing what you "see with the eyes of faith." (15 minutes)
- **Oratio**/Speaking: Speak to God, pray to God—Experience the God-illuminated word as a means to bless and transform the thoughts and images that God's Word has awakened in you. Prayerfully give to God what you have found in your heart. (5 minutes)
- **Contemplatio**/Contemplating: Hear the Word proclaimed again. Notice the transforming presence of God within you. Surrender all that is stirring, if only briefly, and rest in God's embrace. (10 minutes)
- **Conversatio**/Becoming Christ-like: Return to God's word. How is your "way of life" impacted by "seeing and hearing" the word of God

today? How does God want you to be different today as a result of this encounter? (10 minutes)

A facilitator guides the group through the process. These sharing guidelines are important for group functioning.

1. Honor the Spirit of God working through and in the group as the ultimate source of inspiration and growth.
2. Listen to one another. Provide space between each person's sharing. Allow each person to share in the discussion before speaking a second time so that no one becomes a spectator.
3. Listen to others without trying to give advice. Respect differences of opinions without insisting that others agree with your position.
4. Each participant should share from their own perspective and experience. Using the word "I" typically ensures this and prevents participants from speaking on behalf of other people or as if their sharing is a "fact".
5. Allow for a diversity of sharing and viewpoints.
6. Share to the extent that is pertinent to the conversation at hand.

This journal invites you to put your story in conversation with God's story as well as the stories of your companions. As you record your thoughts, feelings, and prayers, you will become more attentive to God's movement in your life. Another source of companionship in this journal are the stories of seasoned ecclesial ministers as they illuminate their ministerial experiences. The intersection of these stories—yours, God's, and the ministers—should encourage fruitful conversation. Your challenge will be twofold: to find your voice and to hear the voice of God. This will take some silent time listening to God. Resist the temptation to run away from the silence. This silence should lead you naturally into conversation and your commitment to follow where Christ leads. You will find more than enough inspiration in each session.

The goal is not to cover everything in the journal but to ruminate on its contents and savor that which settles in you. You may find the last two pieces of each chapter, the reflection on the illuminated word and connecting the charism, something to take with you for your individual exploration. Let them linger with you.

HOSPITALITY

The Story

"Never turn away from the hope which the Gospel offers; now you must not only listen to God's word but also preach it. Hold the mystery of faith with a clear conscience. Express in action what you proclaim by word of mouth. Then the people of Christ, brought to life by the Spirit, will be an offering God accepts. Finally, on the last day, when you go to meet the Lord, you will hear him say: 'Well done, good and faithful servant, enter into the joy of your Lord.'"[1] These words rang in my ears as I knelt before Bishop John Kinney at my ordination to the diaconate. While all eyes were prayerfully on me, it was my son Sam who I wanted to glance at, to get a sense of affirmation and acceptance of my vocational journey.

Although he didn't know it, it was Sam who helped me gain insight into what I proclaim Sunday after Sunday and, more importantly, to express that message in action. His "instruction" began one Holy Saturday as our family waited with great anticipation for the start of the liturgical riches that surround the celebration of the Resurrection. I heard Sam sniffling and thought it was a runny nose, but when I looked over I saw him wiping tears from his eyes. My wife, Mary Beth, leaned over and asked him what was wrong. He replied, "Nothing." But the tears didn't stop. Mary Beth kept asking him what was wrong, and after much prodding he finally responded, "I am just so happy that Jesus doesn't have to suffer anymore!" Bam! I was jolted by his deep compassion.

[1] *The Rite of Ordination: Diaconate, Priesthood.* Collegeville, Minn.: Liturgical, 1969.

His statement struck at the core of my heart and soul as I wondered how he had gained such a heartfelt understanding of the greatness of this Christian event. Deep inside Sam understood the pain and suffering that Jesus went through in the Crucifixion. He understood it, and the only way he could express himself was with weeping.

Flash forward eight years. Sam is now a teenager. He was messy and disorganized and typically grunted to requests from my wife or me for anything we asked of him. He had little zeal for church or liturgy. He seemed like a typical teenager in many ways with one exception—his generous heart with his friends.

I must admit that this was a rub between Sam and me. His friends always seemed a bit rough around the edges and never seemed to me to be the "right" sort of people for Sam. They weren't the role models I wanted for him. But Sam being Sam, he still hung around with them. I couldn't understand why, even though I often pressed him with questions. One friend in particular bugged me. His name was Pete. Sam would invite him over to play video games or to join us for supper. From my perspective, Pete had nothing going for him. He seemed lazy, unmotivated, and had no drive or ambition in life. Yet, Sam loved to spend time with Pete and seemed happiest when he was around. He was always asking to invite him for a meal, to swim in the pool, whatever: Sam wanted to make room for Pete in our family.

One day, Sam asked if we might have a birthday party for Pete who had never had one. Both my wife and I looked at each other wondering how his parents might feel at our usurping their parental responsibility. Sam persisted. We asked him why we should host this party. Sam explained that Pete's parents weren't as lucky as us. What money they made was spent on bare essentials for survival. Sam said that there were times he would visit at Pete's house, and there wouldn't be food in the refrigerator. He insisted that everyone should have a birthday party at least once in their life and that it shouldn't matter if he was our kid or not. Bam! Another jolt!

Sam's persistence won out. We had a big birthday party for Pete—complete with family, friends, birthday gifts, dinner and a cake with candles. You could see on Pete's face that he was moved by the occasion. We sang "Happy Birthday," he blew out candles and opened his presents slowly and meticulously as if each one were a unique treasure. My uneasiness about Pete, however, didn't go away. Soon after that party, I asked Sam again, "Why do you befriend people like Pete?" He said, "Dad, it's because they have nothing. I have everything—food in the refrigerator, clothes not purchased from a thrift store, a nice home, and great parents. I have been given a good life, and I think sometimes I am spoiled. I just want my friends to feel welcomed and we can do this. And besides, you are becoming a deacon . . . and you *have* to do this. It's your job." Bam!

Somewhere along the way Sam discovered a deep understanding about welcoming into his world of comfort and family love people who have fewer material goods than he does. He "gets" what being hospitable means to all who enter his life. Who they are as persons is more important than what they have or what he "gets" from them. He sees beyond the externals of their individual lives and appearances. Sam has the open arms of God—welcoming all without conditions.

These lessons radically moved me to incorporate an understanding of hospitality so natural to Sam. At that Easter Vigil, Sam welcomed into his heart the Holy Spirit who led him to a deep understanding of the pain of rejection Christ experienced. He understood, in his terms, all that Christ did for him and how painful Christ's suffering and death must have been. He knew what it meant to live in the joy of resurrection and as a disciple. He lived that same spirit with all those he met, like the Petes who are always welcome into his life. He doesn't see limitations as I do; he simply extends an unconditional love. I want to believe that in some way Sam connected his experience at the Vigil years before with his commitment to overcome rejection whenever and with whomever he could. Sam became teacher to me in a way of life that I would need to embrace if I were to be ready to be a deacon. I realized that I would not become a deacon just by being ordained anymore than I would become a car mechanic by driving my car into a garage. I needed to put on Christ. Like Sam, I needed to pour out unconditional love to all people regardless of wealth, poverty, race or gender like Jesus did on the cross. I needed to tear down the boundaries I had placed on God's love.

In what ways does your own experience with hospitality connect with this story?

How does this story shape your vocational call?

What does hearing this story with "the ear of the heart" illuminate in you as you explore the practice of ministry?

Suffering Servant
Isaiah 53:2-10

For he grew up before him like a young plant,
  and like a root out of dry ground;
he had no form or majesty that we should look at him,
  nothing in his appearance that we should desire him.
He was despised and rejected by others;
  a man of suffering and acquainted with infirmity;
and as one from whom others hide their faces
  he was despised, and we held him of no account.

Surely he has borne our infirmities
  and carried our diseases;
yet we accounted him stricken,
  struck down by God, and afflicted.
But he was wounded for our transgressions,
  crushed for our iniquities;
upon him was the punishment that made us whole,
  and by his bruises we are healed.
All we like sheep have gone astray;
  we have all turned to our own way,
and the LORD has laid on him the iniquity of us all.

He was oppressed, and he was afflicted,
  yet he did not open his mouth;
like a lamb that is led to the slaughter,
  and like a sheep that before its shearers is silent,
  so he did not open his mouth.
By a perversion of justice he was taken away.
  Who could have imagined his future?
For he was cut off from the land of the living,
  stricken for the transgression of my people.
They made his grave with the wicked
  and his tomb with the rich,

although he had done no violence,
  and there was no deceit in his mouth.

Yet it was the will of the LORD
  to crush him with pain.
When you make his life an offering for sin,
  he shall see his offspring, and shall prolong his days;
through him the will of the LORD shall prosper.

Suffering Servant, Donald Jackson, 2005, *The Saint John's Bible*, Hill Museum & Manuscript Library, Order of Saint Benedict, Collegeville, Minnesota, USA.

AND
HE HELD HIM
OF NO ACCOUNT
SURELY
HE HAS BORNE
OUR INFIRMITIES
AND CARRIED
OUR DISEASES
YET WE ACCOUNTED
HIM STRICKEN
STRUCK DOWN
BY GOD
AND AFFLICTED
BUT HE WAS
WOUNDED
FOR OUR
TRANSGRESSIONS
CRUSHED FOR
OUR INIQUITIES
UPON HIM
WAS THE
PUNISHMENT
THAT MADE
US WHOLE
AND BY
HIS BRUISES
WE ARE
HEALED
ALL WE LIKE
SHEEP HAVE
GONE ASTRAY
WE HAVE ALL
TURNED TO
OUR OWN WAY
AND THE LORD
HAS LAID ON HIM
THE INIQUITY
OF US ALL
HE WAS
OPPRESSED
AND HE WAS
AFFLICTED
YET HE DID NOT
OPEN HIS MOUTH
LIKE A LAMB
THAT IS LED
TO THE
SLAUGHTER
AND LIKE A SHEEP
THAT BEFORE
ITS SHEARERS
IS SILENT
SO HE DID
NOT OPEN
HIS MOUTH

Reflection on the Illuminated Word

This passage from Isaiah captures the relationship between Emmanuel and all God's people. The illumination visualizes the consequences of imprisoning or cutting ourselves off from seeing God in each and every person. In this illumination, there is nothing that is beautiful about the dark figure, secluded and placed in the confinement of his or her surroundings. He is unreachable behind those prison bars. There was nothing that made me look at Pete as having any kind of stateliness—nothing that convinced me to want my son to have him as his friend. In my mind, Pete's appearance and surroundings were shabby and offered little to assure me that he would be a good companion for my son. I had imprisoned Sam's friend by my prejudices, dislikes, and lack of understanding.

Do I have the right person in prison? Was *I* the one imprisoned, standing behind the bars of safety to view what I wanted to ignore or avoid? The image of the dark figure becomes me, hiding from contact with people who fall outside my comfort zone or who fail to meet my criteria or worthiness. This creates a dark place where one can prefer the comforting assurances of safety and security over the risks of ministry and mission.

In the illumination, the dark figure is shackled to the bars of the cell. Those shackles and their chains represent the constraints keeping one from venturing too far out in ministerial situations. They limit the extent to which we might express or receive God's love with individuals or events. Those shackles become a source of security, insuring we don't take too many risks or get too close in relationships where we are not fully in control.

Centered and at the top of the illumination are the golden crosses, denoting God's love. It is a love so powerful that it breaks what binds us. It is a love that penetrates the darkest clouds of life's fears and anxieties. It is God's love which we strive to experience in order that we might move beyond what keeps us safe and sound in the comfortable life we have created. Despite a deep human need for security, God's love challenges us to experience the vast expanses of unknown realities within new and complex relationships in ministry.

Daily we make the decision to either turn from people or to let them in our lives. Sometimes we rely on our own safe places of understanding without taking the risk of encountering Christ, especially in those we most seek to avoid. In fear, we pre-judge what will happen in encounters that don't quite "fit" into our world of comfort or personal need. Sometimes ministry becomes objectified with mission statements, goals and objectives. Left unchecked those useful resources can take precedence over transformational ministry. Ministry may dangerously become sterile and limited rather than relational. We end up dancing around the deep human elements of ministerial experience, explaining relationships but never fully engaging them.

Jesus lived as a member of Jewish society. In that context, he challenged all who followed him to expand their understanding of hospitality, of welcoming all into his Kingdom. For Jesus, this always began with a change of heart. In baptism, each of us receives the Light of Christ and becomes a herald of the Gospel whose challenge never ends: Believe what you read, teach what you believe, and practice what you teach.

Who do you know that is cut off from the land of the living and stricken for the transgression of the community and society? What are ways you look out for the well-being of others: family, friends, and strangers?

Connecting the Charism

Hospitality

"All guests who present themselves are to be welcomed as Christ." Rule of Saint Benedict 53:1

Benedict's guidelines to hospitality underscore the profound respect all human beings merit, evoking behaviors that support, honor and dignify them as though each were Christ being welcomed. By being present in such a radical fashion, we open ourselves to the prophetic role they play. We accept the opportunity to encounter each person with a deep reverence and develop a new and deeper understanding of how Christ's love becomes manifest.

My son seems to do this naturally while I need to cultivate this sense of hospitality with disciplined intention. Perhaps this is the hidden dimension of hospitality we don't readily see in Benedict's instruction or we too quickly pass over its dramatic challenge to us: Accept the stranger as though he or she was Christ himself. It is a brilliant principle as long as the Petes don't show up on your doorstep. When that happens, it is tempting to list all the exceptions you need to make for living by this rule with this person in this instance. But Benedict saw beyond that. He envisioned hospitality which knew no exceptions. His prophetic vision offers the opportunity for Emmanuel to enter one's life in our world with each person encountered.

The ability to be fully engaged in welcoming all with heartfelt generosity has a fearful face, for it challenges us to be vulnerable to others. Hospitality becomes a leap of faith as we open ourselves to someone, giving them permission to create a relationship without strings attached. Each time this occurs, the encounter tests and challenges the delicate web of who we are as well as who we can become. That delicate web is often controlled by what we fear.

To live hospitality with the fullness of our lives opens each of us to the divine mystery of encountering Emmanuel. When we risk that occurrence, we experience a deeper sense of God's presence and love in our lives. We cast our vulnerability aside and trust what it means to belong to the mission of Christ. We become active disciples in our world, not just in thought but also in daily action. As I reflect back on Sam and his friend Pete, I see how Sam's example helped me be far more attentive about accepting people with the heart of Christ. He helped me to embrace my own vulnerability in welcoming the other while discovering ways to become empowered in relationship. What it means to be a loving, welcoming Christian continues to guide my ministry and direct my spiritual growth.

In what ways does your hospitality embody the compassion of God? In what ways do you preserve God's hospitality?

COMMUNITY

The Story

No one prepared us in the seminary for the ragged ways in which parish issues tend to happen. In my naiveté, I thought an issue would arise, people would get together to look at different points of view and options, and then they would make a decision. That was how a Christian community worked—orderly, respectfully, neatly.

Perhaps this was more typical in parish life at one time, perhaps not. Today I know that my time and energy as priest and pastor are spent not so much in the "pastoral care of souls" as in crisis management, personnel issues, and endless meetings for long range planning at both diocesan and local levels. Add to this the particular challenges of leading two parishes recently "twinned" under one pastor, a new model of parish structure that still lacks a clear road map. In some ways we are grieving the loss of parish life as it has been known for some time.

This was dramatized recently by a group of parishioners with some concerns related to the twinning process underway. They asked for a meeting. The trustees and I brought some donuts and put on the coffee. The parishioners brought with them a handout detailing their perceived losses since the two parishes were brought together under one pastor. The notes were entitled "The Beginning of the End." They informed me that when I announced that our bookkeeper would be moving into shared office space at the other parish, it felt like "Their heart was being ripped out." While such deep feelings over a relatively innocent decision are startling, they reflect a process of grieving that requires empathy and patience in equal measure.

Twenty years ago the expectation was that the pastor would spend his time facilitating the work of the parish council and other committees, recruiting good leaders, and supervising a small number of staff personnel. If a parish had more than five hundred families, another priest usually assisted with pastoral care. This model served well for the building up of vibrant parish communities. The personal relationship of people to their pastor was important. Pastors had time to get to know the families with whom they were celebrating baptisms, funerals, weddings, First Communions, Sunday Mass and all the other sacraments. There was always time during a week to visit the sick and elderly as well as teach in the parish grade school if there was one. Currently, administrative responsibilities often trump good pastoral care, and parishioners increasingly feel that all the good work done in building a community with a strong identity is being "undone" with no clear indication of how new models will serve their desire to live out and pass on the faith.

Underneath all of this run streams of anxiety and anger within the Church about the clergy abuse scandal and the related issues of church governance and transparency. We face proposed liturgical changes that for many seem to be a step backward rather than forward. Our financial needs increase even as people's resources are diminished. As a result of these and other factors, pastors get caught in the crossfire of differing opinions, opposing ideas, and feelings of dissatisfaction from many directions. Is this a necessary stage that will yield to growth and good things to come for the future of the Church? Can the grieving, the anger and anxiety all become part of the Paschal Mystery, and bring forth new life for the Church once we come to a "new normal?"

As we grapple with the challenges to community building posed by this new reality, staff colleagues and I try to keep the "big picture" in view—the mission of bringing Christ to the world through preaching and teaching the Good News. It is this mission, not the present perplexities and ambiguities, that will fuel our leadership. I am also keenly aware of the necessity for all of us to gain the skills needed to work closely and collaboratively with parish leaders so that the future that emerges from our common efforts is theirs, and not mine or the staff's.

If the seminary did not prepare pastors for all the messiness of leadership in today's parishes, it did instill a profound respect for the presence of the Holy Spirit moving among God's people. It is the Spirit that gives us wisdom and courage to engage creatively these "new signs of our times."

In what ways does your own experience with community connect with this story?

How does this story shape your vocational call?

What does hearing this story with "the ear of the heart" illuminate in you as you explore the practice of ministry?

The Promise of the Holy Spirit
Acts 1:8

"But you will receive power when the Holy Spirit has come upon you; and you will be my witnesses in Jerusalem, in all Judea and Samaria, and to the ends of the earth."

To the Ends of the Earth, Donald Jackson with contributions from Sally Mae Joseph and Andrew Jamieson, 2002, *The Saint John's Bible*, Hill Museum & Manuscript Library, Order of Saint Benedict, Collegeville, Minnesota, USA.

TO THE
ENDS
OF THE
EARTH

Reflection on the Illuminated Word

This particular illumination is on the final page of the Gospel and Acts volume of *The Saint John's Bible*. It is a picture of the earth as actually seen from space! What a completely different perspective of the "ends of the earth" than in Biblical times when most people traveled fewer than a hundred miles in a lifetime. Even today it is possible to narrow our vision of what it means to be a church sent to the "ends of the earth." One modest effort to expand people's vision of the scope of this instruction from Jesus in this scripture passage is the emergence of global partnerships with faith communities around the world. My own diocese of St. Cloud, Minnesota is in partnership with the Diocese of Homa Bay, Kenya. As a result the clustered parishes of St. Peter and St. Paul in St. Cloud and St. Peter's Parish in Oyugis, Kenya have an on-going relationship. Recently, for example, the youth minister and one of the elementary teachers from St. Cloud have traveled to Kenya to share in the life and ministries of St. Peter's for a month. In turn, a delegation from Homa Bay will be visiting the diocese later this year. Such relationships foster mutual enrichment and encouragement for faith communities and expand the ways members experience a mission that knows no bounds.

Stenciled along the borders of the illumination are crosses. Even in the dramatic and dynamic movement of the planet through space, the Cross of Christ continues to remind us of the vertical (transcendent) and horizontal (incarnational) reaches of our faith. The pattern of crosses speaks to the struggles and sufferings that are a part of taking the Gospel to the ends of the earth and of building Christian community in any corner or place on the earth. The cross, for the believer, is always a sign of hope and not despair. It is a necessary part of the salvation story, leading to Resurrection and Christ's Spirit being poured forth within the Church and upon the world. The Cross speaks to both the grieving and the hope that are present for disciples at any particular era in the life of the church or of a Christian community.

The two parishes described in the story are not separate planets in a vast universe but are a little over a mile down the street from each other. They are living with a mandate from the bishop to cooperate and find new ways of being parish. At one level, this is a practical matter given the limited number of priests available. One pastor for two parishes with a shared staff sounds efficient. Yet, practicality cannot obscure the challenges. Neither parish wants to lose its particular identity, history, and traditions. Both want the pastor's singular attention. Staff from each parish now working as a team find the differences in styles and organizational structures perplexing. This emerging structure is a delicate balance each time parish leadership considers staffing issues, liturgical practices, and even interpersonal relationships.

What this illumination from Acts teaches is that Christian community is dynamic, not static. The energy of this view of the world spills off the page. It cannot be contained or restrained because it is charged with the Spirit. When the Risen Jesus tells the apostles that they are to take the mission to the ends of the earth, he is not offering stability. Even in the world of the early church, such missionary outreach lacked predictability. Return again to the illumination and note what seems to be a dove-shaped cloud penetrating this dynamic visualization of the universe. Then hear the opening of Acts 1:8—"But you will receive power when the Holy Spirit has come upon you, and you will be my witnesses . . ." The command sending the disciples forth into uncharted territory is linked to the promise that they do not venture forward alone.

We are asked to trust in that same presence and power of the Spirit in the very particulars of the ever-present birthing and growing pains involved in being a dynamic church, a church that is never a museum but always a living organism. Some of those particulars in retrospect may be mistakes and errors in judgment, but the clear presence of the cross in the illumination signals a fundamental aspect of Christian life—forgiveness. We need the capacity for forgiveness and willingness to learn from mistakes especially in times of transition and change no matter their source. The Spirit does not abandon us when there are missteps, for the power of the Spirit pierces all darkness for those who trust.

Where have you seen neighboring communities that live as if they are worlds apart? In what ways can you be a bridge-builder?

Connecting the Charism

Community

"The Abbot must not disturb the flock committed to him, nor by an arbitrary use of his power ordain anything unjustly; but let him always think of the account he will have to render to God for all his decisions and his deeds." Rule of St. Benedict 63:1

Paul and the apostles never dealt with the issues of diocesan planning in the face of a "priest shortage" or with clustering of parishes. Early church order, however, was similarly fluid. When the communities dispersed in Acts, they re-grouped significantly different from what they first were. Then and now these new entities represent not merely an organizational issue, for they create new webs of humans interacting and relating. The overarching concerns of building and maintaining Christian community, as well as adapting to new circumstances, are common across centuries.

The idyllic descriptions of Christian community found in Acts tell how they devoted themselves to the apostles' teaching and fellowship, to the breaking of bread and prayer, to the care of anyone in need, and to unity of "one heart and soul." However, the rest of Acts could easily be entitled, "Early Church Squabbles" or "Holy Spirit to the Rescue!" Within these chapters lies our assurance that the anguish, problems and perplexities that we experience today are not completely original, nor need to be our undoing. The instruction we receive from the experience of the first communities is to deal with issues through study, dialogue, and a great deal of reliance upon the Holy Spirit. Whenever a community faced crisis, its members turned (or were turned by their leaders) to the Holy Spirit, always present as the source for direction and courage to move forward.

Then and now, no one has it all together all the time. We are all human beings with our own ideas of what the 'ideal' community should look like. These ideals are heightened in the midst of change and transition. Some agree with the truism that "To live is to change" while many deeply yearn for stability and predictability. Conflicts and discord will always arise within community. The challenge is to recognize and accept the fact that the elusive "ideal community' will never be fully realized this side of Paradise and to commit to the hard work of finding common ground so that the Gospel can be preached in the lives of people striving to live together as though with "one mind and one heart."

As change occurs because of new circumstances or the urgency of mission, parishes and their leaders need first to reflect on the guiding values and principles that will ground their collaboration. Will decisions become merely a matter of financial cost effectiveness? Will discussions end up with the loudest voices getting their way? Will every issue be a battlefield where sides form and the only goal is victory? Or will our efforts to be community even in stressful times find their bearing in concerns for the best possible models of faith formation for young and old, for vibrant worship that equips people for living as disciples of Christ, and for a sense of how we actually become community with generous amounts of prayer, fellowship and justice oriented service? Will we imitate the world where ideological rigidity hardens hearts and minds or will we create a climate where everyone seeks to listen to each other for understanding so that a common ground *for mission* can be forged?

The achievement of such noble goals requires frequent reflection on the teachings of Jesus and on the experience of the early church as it struggled to be faithful and faith-filled. It requires wise and prudent stewardship of financial and human resources. Decisions need to be made in an honest and open, collaborative manner. In all this we can draw on the wisdom of Saint Benedict. In his rule for the monastic community, he reminds those who want to share a common life that "Your way of acting should be different from the world's way; the love of Christ must come before all else. You are not to act in anger or nurse a grudge. Rid your heart of all deceit. Never give a hollow greeting of peace or turn away when someone needs your love."[2] This is the difference between going to church and *being* church and between idealizing community and living as community.

[2] Benedict, and Timothy Fry. "Chapter 4." *RB 1980: The Rule of St. Benedict in English*. Collegeville, Minn.: Liturgical Press, 1982.

How have times of disappointment in the Christian community been doorways to deep belief for you?

LISTENING

The Story

Life as a staff chaplain on an intensive care unit at a large urban hospital requires a lot of listening. Patients in the ICU are often so critically ill that ministry encounters may happen more with their families and friends than with them. These are intense moments that come and go quickly. There are times when I am reminded of the hours I spent as a youth jumping rope because often I feel like I am invited to "jump into" the middle of a person's and their family's story. My experience with Willy, however, reminds me that each time I meet a patient—no matter how long our visit will last and whether or not we will see each other again—it is an "Emmaus moment." It is a time when the Word is mutually broken open as we recognize one another and know the ground on which we stand is indeed holy.

I first met Willy in the ICU unit because he had asked for a chaplain visit. According to his records, he was 59 years old, single, and a transfer from the local Veterans hospital. His next of kin was a daughter living in Cleveland, and he listed his religious preference as Christian. Willy was on a ventilator and could not speak, but his eyes were open and bright. He nodded his head 'yes' and took my hand when I asked if he'd like me to pray with him. I encountered Willy several days later when I was on-call. He had been moved out of the ICU to a private room on another unit. The referral I received simply said, "Requesting chaplain visit; new diagnosis."

When I knocked and entered his room, Willy greeted me with a smile and said, "Hey, you're the one who came to see me when I had that breathing tube in." He added, "I've been here five days now, and yesterday I got the word from the docs that there's nothing more they can do for me. I came here from the VA to get a second opinion. I knew my liver was shot and I was hoping for a liver transplant, but now they've diagnosed me with advanced pancreatic cancer. Like they say, 'It's not over 'til the fat lady sings,' well she's not just humming, she's belting it out."

"I've been doing a lot of thinking since I've been here," he continued. "It's like I've been watching my whole life like a movie. I guess it took something like knowing the end is near before I'd let all the pieces come together. There are so many scenes I'm ashamed of, that I'd edit out." Then as I listened, he began to tell his story.

"I was born in Philly. It was me and my mom and my kid brother, Tim. Our dad left when I was 8 and Tim was 5. It was a relief for all of us when he left. He wasn't what you'd call an ideal father or husband. In the summers when we were little, even before my dad left, Mom would put us on the bus with our aunt and send us down to her mom's in North Carolina. Those summers with my grandma are some of the few truly happy memories I have. She lived in a little town with a creek nearby. I remember she made peach jam and kept her own bees to make honey. Other than wanting to see my Mom again, I never wanted to leave grandma's house. My mom worked two jobs to make ends meet. She was working her night job when the fire broke out and my brother died. He was only 12, still a kid. Everybody told me then that there was nothing I could have done to save him, but I still blame myself for his death.

"So then it was Mom and me. I finished high school but was drafted and sent to Vietnam at 18. It was like I was dropped down onto another planet. I did terrible things there; things I'm afraid not even God can forgive. Not all the pot I smoked there, or the drugs or alcohol I've used since, can wash those memories away.

"I came back and tried community college. I met my wife there and we got married and had two kids. I realize now that I was too screwed up to get married and all I seemed to do was mess up my wife's life. Funny, isn't it? I ended up leaving my family when my son was 8 and my daughter was 5. For so long I hated my old man and then found him looking back at me when I looked in the mirror. I drifted from one odd job to the next. Went as far down into a bottle as a guy could get, and then I kept on pushing the limit of where the bottom really was. I did three stretches in jail for possession and disorderly conduct and finally ended up in prison for a DWI and aggravated manslaughter. Out of boredom one day I went to a Bible study group. I was given a Bible, which is the one I have here."

"What stories in the Bible speak to your heart?" I asked Willy. He said, "I identify totally with the Prodigal Son. My daughter and I have made up, and she's invited me to transfer to the VA in Cleveland so I can be closer to her and her kids. Her forgiveness is greater than health or wealth to me. My wife died when she was 45 years old, killed by a drunk driver. I never got to say goodbye to her, or tell her how sorry I am. The last time I saw my son was at her funeral when he said to me, 'It might as well been you behind the wheel. You're a drunk; you broke her heart; you're the one who really killed her.' I've been sober for five years now. AA has been good for me and I continue to make amends."

Willy and I continued talking and he continued to open the Scriptures to me. He found joy in every lost sheep found, or leper touched, or tax collector called. He identified with all who came to Jesus to be healed. We held hands and prayed together. I left knowing that the Greyhound bus he'd take later that week would bring him to Cleveland, but we both knew that he was heading to Jerusalem, to Golgotha—but that he'd continue on clear to the Resurrection. For my part, I left with my heart burning and my eyes opened.

In what ways does your own experience with listening connect with this story?

How does this story shape your vocational call?

What does hearing this story with "the ear of the heart" illuminate in you as you explore the practice of ministry?

Road to Emmaus
Luke 24:13-35

Now on that same day two of them were going to a village called Emmaus, about seven miles from Jerusalem, and talking with each other about all these things that had happened. While they were talking and discussing, Jesus himself came near and went with them, but their eyes were kept from recognizing him. And he said to them, "What are you discussing with each other while you walk along?" They stood still, looking sad. Then one of them, whose name was Cleopas, answered him, "Are you the only stranger in Jerusalem who does not know the things that have taken place there in these days?" He asked them, "What things?" They replied, "The things about Jesus of Nazareth, who was a prophet mighty in deed and word before God and all the people, and how our chief priests and leaders handed him over to be condemned to death and crucified him. But we had hoped that he was the one to redeem Israel. Yes, and besides all this, it is now the third day since these things took place. Moreover, some women of our group astounded us. They were at the tomb early this morning, and when they did not find his body there, they came back and told us that they had indeed seen a vision of angels who said that he was alive. Some of those who were with us went to the tomb and found it just as the women had said; but they did not see him." Then he said to them, "Oh, how foolish you are, and how slow of heart to believe all that the prophets have declared! Was it not necessary that the Messiah should suffer these things and then enter into his glory?" Then beginning with Moses and all the prophets, he interpreted to them the things about himself in all the scriptures.

As they came near the village to which they were going, he walked ahead as if he were going on. But they urged him strongly, saying, "Stay with us, because it is almost evening and the day is now nearly over." So he went in to stay with them. When he was at the table with them, he took bread, blessed and broke it, and gave it to them. Then their eyes were opened, and they recognized him; and he vanished from their sight. They said to each other, "Were not our hearts burning within us while he was talking to us on the road, while he was opening the scriptures to us?" That same hour they got up and returned to Jerusalem; and they found the eleven and their companions gathered together. They were saying, "The Lord has risen indeed, and he has appeared to Simon!" Then they told what had happened on the road, and how he had been made known to them in the breaking of the bread.

Road to Emmaus, Donald Jackson, 2002, *The Saint John's Bible*, Hill Museum & Manuscript Library, Order of Saint Benedict, Collegeville, Minnesota, USA.

JESUS HIMSELF CAME NEAR
AND WENT WITH THEM
HE TOOK BREAD, BLESSED &
BROKE IT, & GAVE IT TO THEM:
THEN THEIR EYES WERE OPENED,
AND THEY RECOGNIZED HIM;
AND HE VANISHED
FROM THEIR SIGHT.

Reflection on the Illuminated Word

The story of the Road to Emmaus begins with two of the disciples struggling to make sense of their experience of Jesus' death and their gut-wrenching grief and profound sense of loss and gloom. It is easy to imagine what their questions may have been: "We thought for sure he was the Messiah. What happened? Were we duped? How could such hope turn into ashes?" Quietly Jesus comes upon them on the road and begins to walk with them. Jesus asks a simple question: "What are you discussing?" Jesus listens to the disciples' response. We see that it is important to Jesus that he hears of the disciples' experience in their words. Deeply listening to the stories others have to tell is an invitation to be in communion, to listen to the questions and the feelings behind the words that are spoken.

One senses that as Jesus opened the Scriptures to the disciples, both their minds and hearts were flooded with insights and connections. So strong was their sense of rapport with this stranger that they did not want the moment to end. And so they extended an invitation to spend more time together over a meal. We get the feeling that there was nothing extraordinary about their meal setting; nothing was forced or orchestrated. The phrase, "He happened to take bread and utter a blessing; he broke it and offered it to them," carries the sense that such behavior was common fare. Yet in that simple, everyday occurrence a profound epiphany took place. Their eyes were opened and they recognized him. Yet, no sooner did the recognition take place than Jesus vanished from their sight. Rather than being paralyzed or mystified into a dazed inactivity, the two disciples were set afire by Jesus' words and presence. The energy from this encounter with Jesus was too great to be contained in quiet introspection and contemplation. The disciples were impelled to return immediately to the community in Jerusalem to bear witness to the Risen Christ.

In the Illumination of the Road to Emmaus, we see Moses and the prophets on the right side and the Tree of Life from Genesis on the left. Gold—the color indicating God's presence—is richly woven throughout the Illumination. Note that the road itself is golden, which tells us in a pictorial fashion that God is present with us throughout our journeys. The large V-shaped gold section in the upper right hand bears an abstract image of the cross. The road the disciples are traveling—as in each of our journeys—bears the shadow of the cross, indicating the Paschal pattern inherent in each person's life. In the meal scene in the upper left, Jesus is depicted in resplendent gold—his divine nature shines forth. The figure on the left in the dinner scene wears pastel colors that mirror the pastel colors seen in the Christ figure as he first approached the disciples on the road, illustrating how the Divine imprints our own human nature. The small blue crosses on the figure to the right testify to the daily crosses we each carry and bring to the Eucharist. The configuration of Jesus at the table with the two disciples bears a marked similarity to Rublev's icon of the Trinity, which is a reminder that we, too, are invited into the fullness of Trinitarian communion and love.

At the hospital where I work, lunch is a time for the chaplains to gather. It is a time of fellowship, a time to share on a personal and professional level. Frequently one of us will make reference to a recent visit. Always mindful of confidentiality, we share the essence and mystery of these pastoral encounters with awe and respect. The listening presence of the chaplain who received the story moves to a deeper level as she or he recounts how the interaction has deepened his or her own journey of faith. The original story is broken open and its fruits are shared with those gathered round the table. This is the nature of deep listening: It is expansive. The rippling effect of the truth spoken reverberates and has the power to heal all those who have ears to hear. Like the disciples on the Road to Emmaus, we realize that we are not alone. Rather, we belong to the Infinite, and we have blessed work to do.

On your ministerial journey, what have you been discussing? And with whom? Have you found your heart burning, broken, beating, leaping or simply wanting more?

Connecting the Charism

Listening

"The disciple's part is to be silent and to listen. And for that reason if anything has to be asked of the Superior, it should be asked with all the humility and submission inspired by reverence." The Rule of St. Benedict 6

St. Benedict places listening in a privileged location in his Rule—as the first word of his Prologue—and positions it at the heart of what it means to be a monk and a disciple of Jesus Christ. The focus on listening is emphasized repeatedly in the Scripture verses St. Benedict quotes in the Prologue. "If you hear his voice today, do not harden your hearts" (Ps 94[95]:8). "If you have ears to hear, listen . . ." (Rev 2:7) and "Come and listen to me; I will teach you the fear of the Lord" (Ps 33[34]:12). Following Benedict's lead, listening, then, is at the core of my deepening identity as a chaplain, spiritual director and pastoral leader.

When we listen, we are a guest in another person's space. My favorite definition of listening is "to wait in suspense." To be listened to deeply by another liberates, heals and transforms us. Attentive listening is hard work; it takes intention and commitment.

Listening is a choice; we must make a decision to listen to another person. It takes energy to listen; we cannot listen passively. In her book on listening, Kay Lindahl says, "Once we become aware of listening as a choice, we notice that we have many opportunities to practice choosing to listen in our daily lives . . . Listening is also a gift. In fact, listening is one of the greatest gifts we can give another—to listen to him or her with total attention."[3] There is mutuality in the act of listening. The one being listened to and the listener are both nourished by these listening experiences. In a Christian context, when these deep listening interactions are entered into, there is a palpable sense of being in the presence of the Holy—the Spirit is present.

[3] Lindahl, Kay. *Practicing the Sacred Art of Listening: a Guide to Enrich Your Relationships and Kindle Your Spiritual Life—the Listening Center Workshop*. Woodstock, Vt.: SkyLight Paths Pub., 2003.

How can you cultivate this kind of listening? One of best ways is to begin to notice how much noise there is in your life and to begin to find opportunities for silence in your day. In a cultural context where multitasking is praised and being plugged-in 24/7 is promoted, seeking a daily contemplative practice is a counter-cultural move; it also befriends your soul. The day's lectionary readings and centering prayer is the framework of my daily discipline which helps me dwell in silence before the flurry of the day begins.

Along with chaplaincy, I also am a trained spiritual director. In both these ministries emphasis is placed on listening to people's stories especially to the questions that spring both from life's circumstances and also those questions that abide in the deep recesses of the heart. *"My wife and I have been married for 58 years. The first thing we do each and every morning is to make our bed together. How can I make the bed when I soon will be alone?" "I knew my son drank, but so do all young people. He's only 28 years old and now the doctors are telling us he is too sick for a liver transplant. I don't understand how this all happened before our eyes and we didn't see it. How can I ever forgive myself, and how can I forgive him?" "My cancer was in remission for almost two years and now it's back. I prayed so hard asking God to let me live to see my first grandchild. My grandson is almost one year old. My prayer was answered, but now I want more. Am I being ungrateful to ask for more time?"*

There are no pat answers for these kinds of questions; they require only that the listener provide a safe place for their reception. "Negative capability" is a helpful concept that I am frequently reminded of when I confront my own deep questions or when I am entrusted with the deep questions of others. The phrase "negative capability" was first used by the poet John Keats. In contrast with the "positive capability" of understanding and insight, "negative capability" refers to being comfortable with not knowing, and not understanding. It is the ability to be peaceful and comfortable with the mysteries, uncertainties, ambiguities and the "unknowableness" of life. Being with others in their pain means offering to bear witness—through the presence of the listening "ear of my heart"— to the tension that exists between despair and hope.

The turnover of patients on the surgical ICU is rapid. I might have only one or two visits—as was the case with Willie—before we vanish from each other's sight. Over time, meeting and listening to so many people's stories told while they, or their loved one is experiencing incredible stress that major illnesses bring, makes me susceptible to compassion fatigue. This kind of fatigue happens when my gift and joy—being able to listen to others—becomes my cross. I know when I am reaching a limit when I feel beside myself—literally. When I feel ungrounded I know that I need to slow down, to pay attention to what is going on inside me and to face my own vulnerability. I find great support for this inward, reflective listening in my commitment to monthly sessions with my spiritual director. Sometimes I have an image of me being washed up on her door step, dripping wet and panting, but ready to mine my experiences, vulnerabilities and the questions that have accompanied me since our last visit.

My ministerial identity and pastoral leadership comes from a seasoning of my baptismal promises. The more I embrace the same belovedness of God that Jesus heard at his baptism, the more I live into the meaning that I am—as all of us are—a beloved child of God. Leadership flows from knowing to whom I belong. Like so many things that are deep and true, leadership springs much more from the font of being than from specific actions or attributes. "Emmaus moments" are woven into the fabric of our days. Leadership comes when we have the ears, heart, and wisdom to listen.

How does listening express itself in your life these days?

REVERENCE FOR ALL PERSONS

The Story

The two fifth grade boys stood sheepishly in my principal's office dressed in heavy coats, hats, mittens, snowpants and boots. Their red cheeks showed the twenty-degree January temperature. The playground supervisor had sent them to me for a serious infraction—bullying a first grader. They knew that David had a quick temper, and they apparently had taken pleasure in stirring it up that day. "Peter and Greg, what were you two thinking? You are fifth graders; you are supposed to be the example at St. Philip's School." No response from either of them. "I will need to think about the consequences. Tomorrow at recess, report to the office."

Yes, I really needed to think. David wasn't just any first grade student. He was our only Hispanic student, but I didn't think that the action was racially motivated. David had had a particularly difficult kindergarten year. He was a frequent "visitor" to the office because of his acting out. His kindergarten teacher was determined to help him gain control of himself so he could succeed. His mother knew he was a smart boy and wanted him to be good. We were definitely partners in our efforts.

St. Phillip's is a small school with only six classrooms and teachers. Sometimes, while on recess duty, the other teachers saw David's stubbornness, but they seldom saw his warm side. Some of them thought he should be asked to leave. Was it racial? I didn't want to think so. I was determined, though, not to let him fall through the cracks. We had good rapport probably because we spent so much time together working things out. Some of the other teachers thought he was getting preferential treatment. I saw it as him getting what he needed; fair is not always equal. When David entered first grade, his mother decided to try medication to help him gain control, and it worked. He could concentrate and was getting along quite well with the new teacher.

But now this. What was I to do with the fifth-grade bullies? Lunch period followed recess and the incident found its way to the teachers' lounge. As usual, they saw David as the source of the problem. Peter and Greg needed to be outside, they said, not staying in from recess. The definite implication was for me not to overreact.

Whatever decision I made would find its critics, but my nine years as principal taught me that was usually the case. As the leader of the school community, I needed to reverence all those involved: the instigators, the victim, the teachers and the parents. The action of these boys had disrupted the community of our school. How could they make up for the disrespect they had shown?

After school, I was outside supervising the bus lines. "Walk. The sidewalks are very icy," I kept repeating to the students who were so anxious to head home. That was it! There was my answer! I went back into the school and found the ice chopping spades. My two strong fifth graders could spend recess for the next two days chopping ice.

The next day, right at 11:10 a.m., Peter and Greg reported to the office. The weather had warmed up a bit, and the stubborn sheet of ice was beginning to loosen a little. I handed each of them an ice chopper and told them how they were going to help our school community by making the sidewalks safer. They didn't argue at all but went right to work. I watched from the window as they chopped and scraped for the next twenty minutes. The next day it was the same story. No complaining. Steady ice chopping. And at the end, I praised them for their good attitude and the positive contribution they had made to our school.

As fortune would have it, the next week it was David being sent in from recess to the office. Second-grader Paul was with him, blood dripping from his nose. After I took care of the bleeding, David and I had our talk. "This is very serious business. You can't fight on the playground. Is this any way to treat your friends here at St. Philip's?" David replied, "We were wrestling, and he was holding down my arms. The only way I could get away was to head-butt him." I kept my stern principal face and gave my favorite response, "I will need to think about the consequences for this. Come down to the office tomorrow at recess time." David burst into tears and sobbed, "Don't make me chop ice." "We shall see," I replied.

The next day at recess, I met David with the ice chopping spade. He cried all the way to the door. This time I went outside too, carrying a shovel. We went to the back door so that he would be out of the sight of the other students. He needed encouragement and reassurance, so as he chopped and I shoveled away the ice, I told him what a good job he was doing and how much safer it would be now for his teacher who used that door every morning. We talked about how to get along with others and how every person deserved respect because we are all God's children. After fifteen minutes, he skipped off to recess for the last five minutes as I carried the shovel and chopper into the school.

A principal can never be really sure if her decisions are the best ones. I kept wondering, had it really been bullying? Were the teachers right and I was overreacting? Did the fifth graders learn from the experience? Would they and David now have greater respect for their fellow students?

A few days later, I was invited to the fifth grade classroom to listen to them read the essays they had written for Catholic Schools Week. The week's theme was "Catholic Schools: Dividends for Life." I heard the answer to my concern as Peter read:

"We at St. Philip School get a good education. We learn how to share here, not bully. If we bully, we chip ice which is a good punishment. Some of the things we share are love, friendship, knowledge, faith, the Ten Commandments and many more . . . And if we learn anything it's to share, have fun and love God. We try to remember that God loves us all the same. So remember this: JOY—Jesus, others, yourself. If you put people in this order you will be happy."

In what ways does your own experience with reverencing all people connect with this story?

How does this story shape your vocational call?

What does hearing this story with "the ear of the heart" illuminate in you as you explore the practice of ministry?

Wisdom Woman
Wisdom 7:22b-30

There is in her a spirit that is intelligent, holy,
unique, manifold, subtle,
mobile, clear, unpolluted,
distinct, invulnerable, loving the good, keen,
irresistible, beneficent, humane,
steadfast, sure, free from anxiety,
all-powerful, overseeing all,
and penetrating through all spirits
that are intelligent, pure, and altogether subtle.
For wisdom is more mobile than any motion;
because of her pureness she pervades and penetrates all things.
For she is a breath of the power of God,
and a pure emanation of the glory of the Almighty;
therefore nothing defiled gains entrance into her.
For she is a reflection of eternal light,
a spotless mirror of the working of God,
and an image of his goodness.
Although she is but one, she can do all things,
and while remaining in herself, she renews all things;
in every generation she passes into holy souls
and makes them friends of God, and prophets;
for God loves nothing so much as the person who lives with wisdom.
She is more beautiful than the sun,
and excels every constellation of the stars.
Compared with the light she is found to be superior,
for it is succeeded by the night,
but against wisdom evil does not prevail.

Wisdom Woman, Donald Jackson, 2006, *The Saint John's Bible*, Hill Museum & Manuscript Library, Order of Saint Benedict, Collegeville, Minnesota, USA.

she who knows your works
and was present when you made the world;
she understands what is pleasing in your sight
and what is right according to
your commandments.
10 Send her forth from the holy heavens,
and from the throne of your glory send her,
that she may labor at my side,
and that I may learn what is pleasing to you.
11 For she knows and understands all things,
and she will guide me wisely in my actions
and guard me with her glory.
12 Then my works will be acceptable,
and I shall judge your people justly,
and shall be worthy of the throne
of my father.
13 For who can learn the counsel of God?
Or who can discern what the Lord wills?
14 For the reasoning of mortals is worthless,
and our designs are likely to fail;
15 for a perishable body weighs down the soul,
and the earthy tent burdens the
thoughtful mind.
16 We can hardly guess at what is on earth,
and what is at hand we find with labor;
but who has traced out what is in the heavens?
17 Who has learned your counsel,
unless you have given wisdom
and sent your holy spirit from on high?
18 And thus the paths of those on
earth were set right,
and people were taught what pleases you,
and were saved by wisdom."

10

Wisdom protected the first-formed father of the
world, when he alone had been created;
she delivered him from his transgression,
2 and gave him strength to rule all things.

Reflection on the Illuminated Word

Solomon considered well when God said to him, "Ask something of me and I will give it to you" (1 Kgs 3:5). When undertaking his leadership role as the new king of Israel, what did he need most? Riches? Power? Popularity? No, he asked for an understanding heart, for wisdom (1 Kgs 3:9).

Every day as I drive to school, I pray for that same gift. Master's degrees and administrative licensure prepare one to be a school principal functionally, but it is wisdom that prepares one to lead. Among the seven headings and thirty-four subheadings on my job description as Catholic school principal, one jumps off the page: "The principal fosters quality interpersonal relationships in an atmosphere of Christian love and concern." How could this be possible without wisdom?

Quality interpersonal relationships begin with reverence for each person in the community. Anytime we are working with people and many personalities, it is a masterful leader who can encourage others in taking responsibility to get along. Every action of leadership is like the stone thrown into the pond, sending rippling circles into the school, parish and town communities. Some decisions are as mundane as which paper to purchase, and some are as life-influencing as the proper punishment for two fifth graders trying out some bully tactics on a first grader.

As we look into the mirror of the illumination of the Wisdom Woman, we see a face that reveals vast experience. Surrounded by cosmic images and the phases of the moon, she shows years of interaction with God's creation, reflecting back the image of God's goodness. Though weathered by life's daily challenges and trials, she maintains a gentle smile which seems to say that she has not burned out nor let negativity overwhelm her. She truly shows a spirit that is "not baneful, loving the good, keen, unhampered, beneficent, kindly, firm, secure, tranquil" (Wis 7:22b).

This Wisdom Woman of the illumination inspires a confidence that she would be a willing listener and find gentle truth to share. Most parents today are looking for that listener and the understanding heart of Solomon when they visit with me or one of the teachers. In the small families with one or two children that are so prevalent today, parents often tend to hover over their children. They want to know all that is happening, and they want direct input in their children's education. Sometimes their interest is positive, sometimes not. During times of meeting with disappointed or angry parents, the principal needs the wisdom that is "clear, unstained, certain." The calm confidence of the Wisdom Woman can help lead to the prudence and fortitude needed to find truth while respecting the parent and jointly searching for common ground based on the teachings of Jesus.

Wisdom helps us consider the value of each person in our decision making. Yet, we strive to look at them, not as the world does, but as God would have us. Who gets our first consideration? Is it the leader of the town or the wealthy doctor? Do we think first of the reaction of the "squeaky wheel" who will be on the telephone to much of the town as soon as the decision is made? Or do we risk their displeasure by giving equal consideration to the first grade Hispanic boy with the single mom?

As I looked at David and the fifth graders that winter day, I found myself thinking, "Whose opinion do I fear as I decide upon my course of action? Was I willing to take on the disdain of some teachers in order to respect this first grader? Did I want to risk the arguments that usually come from fifth grade boys? Was I willing to take the accusation of playing favorites?" In the grand scheme of things, this was a small matter, but, then, life is made up of a series of mostly small matters. Character building happens one small step at a time. Building a community of Christian love and concern requires reverence for all persons even though at times this does not always make everyone happy.

Has the Wisdom Woman in the illumination mastered all the aspects of Wisdom? I think not. But she appears firm and secure, knowing that her decisions are made from a godly perspective and this is enough. God calls us to leadership not because we are perfect in all our actions and decisions, but because He wishes to work through us. Where do we begin? We must start by growing our own holiness. The necessity of daily prayer, peaceful meditation, and space for quiet and reflection are never clearer than when a parish leader begins to see that the busyness of church work is getting in the way of her relationship with God. It is easy to say that we must take time to spend with God, but then who will go through the pile of papers on the desk or finish the budget or plan the calendar? These are the times that test how much we really trust the words of Jesus. When he said, "Give and gifts will be given to you; a good measure, packed together, shaken down, and overflowing, will be poured into your lap" (Luke 6:38), is he also speaking about our gift of time? If we give time to Him, will He not also give us time for the bills, the budget and the calendar?

"Wisdom produces friends of God and prophets." To be a parish leader can be an overwhelming challenge. Still, confidence in the God who called us to service and constant prayer for the wisdom required to reverence each person in our care enable us to undertake the job with the quiet confidence of the Wisdom Woman.

Who do you see when you look in the mirror? How has that image developed over your lifetime?

Connecting the Charism

Reverence for All Persons

"No one is to pursue what he judges better for himself, but instead, what he judges better for someone else." The Rule of St. Benedict 72

"I'm first!" Elementary teachers hear that phrase dozens of times a day. Children rush and push to be first in line. They want to be the first to have a turn in a game or the first to get the birthday treat. Some even want to be the first to finish a test even if it means half the answers are wrong. There is something addictive about the need to always be first.

Children are not alone, however, in wanting to be first. Television ads tell us we need to be the first to have the new car or the most popular clothes or the biggest diamond. Parents want their children to be the first on the baseball team or the first in their class. It seems to be part of our human nature to want to be drawn into the first half of St. Paul's teaching (Rom 12:10): "They should each try to be the first . . ." And then startled as one reads the complete sentence: . . . "the first to show respect to the other."

The religion series at my elementary school bears the title, *Image of God.* Our students hear this phrase every year they are with us: "You are an image of God." We emphasize with them that God made all of us. He loves each of us. We care for each other because we are all images of God. In this context, the words of St. Paul make complete sense. We should be the first to show respect for the other because the other is also a beloved child of God, made in his image and deserving of our love as fellow members of God's family.

St. Benedict challenges us to go one step further when he writes, "No one is to pursue what he judges better for himself, but instead, what he judges better for someone else"[4] It is not enough to just hold the other in the same esteem as ourselves. Rather, we are to put the other first. To live and teach this is completely counter-cultural in contemporary society. It probably was in the time of St. Benedict as well.

[4] Benedict, and Timothy Fry. "Chapter 72." *RB 1980: The Rule of St. Benedict in English*. Collegeville, Minn.: Liturgical Press, 1982.

Hopefully, this way of putting others first begins at home when the toddler first realizes that he can say "no." In kindergarten, we call it sharing and being kind. When the students shove their way into line, they go back to the carpet and try again. If one student demands the last chocolate cupcake that was just taken by the girl in front of her because she doesn't want white, she will probably be made to wait until last or have none at all. Giving students the opportunity to sing for the nursing home residents or clean up the parish cemetery helps them learn to think of others and their needs. With consistent reinforcement, the children begin to realize what it means to have reverence for each person. Taking turns is still a challenge, but eventually most students begin to look out for each other.

There are children, however, who grow into adulthood never having learned this important lesson. Often, they resort to making themselves first by putting others down. On the playground and the school bus, it may start with name calling and teasing. As these children become adults and start climbing the ladder of success, it may mean stepping on as many others as necessary on the way to the top. During hard economic times, the difference in attitude toward others can be especially evident. Some don't care how many get laid off as long as they keep their own positions and benefits. Then there are others who vote to cut back their own hours or pay so that no one loses a job.

One of the challenges in first considering what is best for the other is that there are so many "others" to think about, and they often have conflicting needs. When my two fifth graders were sent to the office, they obviously had been thinking about what would be the most entertaining for themselves rather than what was best for David. When I contemplated the consequence for their behavior, I needed to weigh the needs of Peter and Greg, but also what was best for David, the teachers, and the rest of the school community. I needed to be sure that I was not thinking first of what would be easiest for me. I could have given a verbal reprimand and let it go at that: easy for me, comfortable for most of the teachers, but not good for David or the fifth graders.

Here lies the biggest challenge in leadership: how to make the best decision while reverencing all the persons involved. This is when we humbly pray for wisdom to consider all that is at stake, listen to the words of Jesus about what it means to live in right relationship with one another, and then let God work through us as we courageously act.

When have you had the courage to do something unconventional to express your faith in God?

JUSTICE

The Story

The fiery orange light of the early morning sunrise washed over my kitchen walls as I got breakfast on and packed lunches for the kids, except for our three year old. I could feel that it was going to be a great day. After the kids left to catch the school bus, my husband came in from milking the cows. At the table he sullenly asked, "So you're really gonna do it?" "It" was participating in a demonstration for peace in front of Honeywell Corporation Headquarters in the Cities with a group of Franciscan Sisters and others from the area.

"Yes, I am. I have to do this. It's hard to explain . . . I just know I have to."

He ate in silence as I checked my to-do list. Satisfied, I grabbed my bag, kissed him and our daughter good-bye, wished them a good day, and headed for the door. "If you get arrested," he barked after me, "don't call me for bail!"

Thus began my first experience of working for peace on the frontline. About a year later I traveled by bus with some of the same Franciscans to Washington, D.C., to participate in the Peace Ribbon March around the Pentagon. This time my leave-taking wasn't quite so difficult. What touched me most at this event was standing with an estimated fifteen to twenty thousand people of like mind and heart as each group unfurled banners to chants of 'Peace for the world' and 'No more war.' I had no doubts about being there; my heart knew it was right.

More recently after the invasion of Afghanistan, I joined a local peace and justice group. I had a personal stake in what was going on in that part of the world since my youngest daughter was a U.S. Navy sailor aboard an aircraft carrier in the Gulf. When the buildup for the invasion of Iraq began, our group started demonstrating for peace downtown. I chose to position myself along the street in front of my parish rectory, protesting my pastor's support of the government's plans. I truly believed war was not the answer to problems among nations.

Being on the picket line was not easy, especially in our town located close to the National Guard Camp Ripley, which made a sizeable economic contribution to the local economy. Many townspeople had family or friends in the Guard and/or were employed there. In our first days of protesting on street corners, hardly anybody showed any sign of support. More typically, passing drivers called out insults punctuated many times with obscene gestures. Sometimes an irate driver would pull over and come out for a face-to-face confrontation on the sidewalk. Most of the time, he or she would say they supported the impending invasion because of 9/11. When we counter-argued that Iraq had nothing to do with 9/11, we seemed to succeed somewhat in getting people to think a bit more about the issues and not react solely to fear-based media.

Thankfully, there also were people who gave us a "thumbs up" and waved as they passed. These were the folks whose support encouraged us to keep coming back every week. As weeks turned into months with no end of the conflict in sight, we noticed more honks and fewer insults. Nobody expected our troops to be on the ground that long. My daughter was in the Gulf for the invasion of Iraq, and while I drew comfort from the fact that she was not in direct danger, no one could have been happier than I when her carrier docked stateside several months later.

Over the years I came to understand the source within me that led to my overt actions for peace. It began in 1973 with the accidental drowning of our second child, not yet two years old, in the creek just a short distance down the road from our farm. My idyllic world instantly shattered and would never again be the same. For my husband of solid German stock, the funeral marked the end: our son was dead. For him, it was time to move on. I was too choked with grief to talk about it so our loss became an 'unmentionable' in our relationship.

Almost five years later I was blessed with a profound experience of God during an altar call at a parish mission. It truly brought light and peace into my heavy heart. Somehow God touched me and filled me with indescribable joy. I came to life again! Even though I had never asked aloud, "If God loves me, why did God take my son?" the question must have been in my heart. But that night God convinced me of God's tender and undying love for me. From then on what mattered to me was to respond to God's love. Slowly I began to realize that God loves *each person* as much as me; and if God loves them, then I should, too. I learned about the brother- and sisterhood of humanity—and of creation—from my Franciscan friends. I began to take seriously the words of the Peace Prayer of St. Francis: "Lord, make me an instrument of your peace . . ." In time I became an Associate of the Franciscan Sisters of Little Falls and work for them today in their Office for Associates.

One of the unforeseen joys of my actions for peace was seeing the effect they had on my husband. Perhaps the truism about mellowing with age played into it, but eventually he came around to accepting my activism. He didn't join me in demonstrating or writing letters to the editor, but his hostility disappeared. He listened intently to the stories I'd tell over supper about things that happened at the peace demonstrations in town. He often started supper on those nights, knowing I'd be getting home later than usual. We somehow had learned to balance the demands of justice—the call to action and the challenge to comprehend that which we don't fully understand.

In what ways does your own experience with justice connect with this story?

How does this story shape your vocational call?

What does hearing this story with "the ear of the heart" illuminate in you as you explore the practice of ministry?

Word Made Flesh
John 1:1–14

In the beginning was the Word, and the Word was with God, and the Word was God. He was in the beginning with God. All things came into being through him, and without him not one thing came into being. What has come into being in him was life, and the life was the light of all people. The light shines in the darkness, and the darkness did not overcome it.

There was a man sent from God, whose name was John. He came as a witness to testify to the light, so that all might believe through him. He himself was not the light, but he came to testify to the light. The true light, which enlightens everyone, was coming into the world.

He was in the world, and the world came into being through him; yet the world did not know him. He came to what was his own, and his own people did not accept him. But to all who received him, who believed in his name, he gave power to become children of God, who were born, not of blood or of the will of the flesh or of the will of man, but of God.

And the Word became flesh and lived among us, and we have seen his glory, the glory as of a father's only son, full of grace and truth.

Word Made Flesh, Donald Jackson, 2002, *The Saint John's Bible*, Hill Museum & Manuscript Library, Order of Saint Benedict, Collegeville, Minnesota, USA.

AND THE WORD BECAME FLESH
AND LIVED AMONG US

Reflection on the Illuminated Word

What immediately captures one's attention is the golden larger-than-life figure stepping across a threshold: the Word—God—become human, crossing from eternity into time. We know the figure is Jesus. His transparent body allows the light of God's life and love to shine through him upon all creation. John points to the light of Christ, pressing the fact that he pointed to the light but was clearly subordinate to it.

Jesus, in presenting himself to the "world," and especially to "his own," the Jewish people, was met with ignorance and rejection. I wanted my life to point to the light of Christ. At times it bore the same ignorance and rejection. It became apparent that the cross of Christ carried light and darkness at the same time. Crosses are portrayed as both light and dark in this illumination; however, there is one cross that is undeniably gold and filled with light. It is the partial cross protruding from behind Jesus' head witnessing to the Evangelist's belief that the cross was the instrument of Jesus' glory and triumph over the darkness of sin and death. The multiple small crosses suggest that crosses are part and parcel of human life. To be a Christian is to be willing to carry one's cross as Jesus did. Generally, we do not have a choice in the cross we bear. I certainly never opted for losing a child. Neither was it my intention to cause a rift between my husband and me by my involvement with actions for peace and justice. However, when the Spirit calls, one must respond . . . or spend enormous amounts of effort trying to evade the call. But with the answering comes the courage to do what needs to be done. In the illumination, most of the crosses are in the light, telling us that Jesus is there to help us carry them (cf. Matt 11:29-30). I, like John the Baptist, wanted my life to point to Jesus. It was Jesus who held the power to bring people into the truth, to reveal the nature of things through his words and life.

The dark background recalls the opening verse of Genesis: "In the beginning when God created the heavens and the earth, the earth was a formless void and darkness covered the face of the deep" (Gen 1:1). The darkness is also overcome by the light brought into the world by Jesus. Although biblical darkness conjures up images of discord and evil, I also see its potential: The pregnant darkness out of which all creation was birthed as was Jesus from the darkness of his mother's womb. Is the female figure standing beside him on his right his Mother Mary, whose hand Jesus is grasping? And is the book in his left hand the Torah in which his coming was foretold through the ages? God's covenants with humanity are recorded there too, as well as the human responses at times challenged by the prophets.

In the Franciscan tradition, the Incarnation takes center place as the clearest revelation of God's extravagant love for humankind. Blessed John Duns Scotus, a thirteenth century Franciscan theologian, taught that for all eternity God planned to become a human being in order to reveal the depth of God's love for us. It builds on an earlier teaching of St. Irenaeus that God's becoming human was not dependent on the creature Adam's sin. Rather, God became human in order to be more fully in relationship with us. In other words, the Incarnation was not God's "Plan B." Humanity's propensity for sin is not diminished or denied in the Franciscan tradition. For Franciscans, however, the emphasis is on God's initiative: God first loves us. Our life's challenge is to respond to that love. As our response deepens, we are transformed as Thomas Aquinas summed up concisely: "For the Son of God became man so that we might become God" (*Opusc.* 57, 1-4)." As God's self-revelation, Jesus remains singular and unique as the only avenue to the Father.

The presentation of Jesus' birth cries out that salvation is at hand. God has overcome sin, and God has come among us in human form. The Incarnation bears witness to the intrinsic goodness of humanity (cf. Gen 1:31). Francis of Assisi embodied Christ in the flesh. During his lifetime the notion of humanity's goodness had pretty much been forgotten. The violence of war and poverty, greed and class strife ruled the land. Even the Church, in word and action, emphasized humanity's sinfulness.

It is easy to get lost in the simple legend of Christmas as Luke portrays it—the inn, the manger, and the shepherds. For many of us, it was the historical presentation of faith. The Son of God comes as man, born in simple circumstances, to save us and bring us home. The Gospel of John tells us that the Word became flesh and lived among us. Christ came to do a job among us. Christ did not become flesh to *observe* us, but to *serve* and thus to *save* us. This takes us beyond a child-like faith.

Francis, the 'little poor man' from Assisi, set about to incarnate the heart of God when he received the call to "Rebuild my house which, as you can see, is falling completely into ruin." Previously he had always tried to avoid these 'undesirables' of society, but on one particular day it was impossible for him to do so. He encountered a leper who propelled him on the road to conversion of heart. He overcame his revulsion, got down off his horse, went over to the leper begging in the roadway and kissed his hand as he gave him a coin. From then on Francis spent much time caring for those unloved and forgotten members of society. He recognized in them the suffering Jesus whom he wanted with all his heart to love and serve. His compassion toward them offered relief from their suffering and strengthened them to carry the crosses which life had given them. From them Francis learned the richness of poverty, that is, total dependence on a loving God who does provide, generously, for our daily needs. Meanwhile, the people of Assisi thought him crazy and spurned his efforts on the part of the poor, much like Jesus was met by rejection and ignorance by "his own" people upon presenting himself to the world.

My call to become active in peace and justice activities resulted from my growing understanding that just as God loves me, so God loves all people, no exceptions. If God's love could be so expansive, my challenge was to strive to do likewise. My leper was politics. I did my patriotic duty by voting, but that was the end of my involvement. With the wars following on the heels of 9/11, I knew I had to start being in touch with my representatives in Congress and state legislators. I could no longer be passive. They needed to hear my point of view, and they did—often. So did the local citizenry who read my letters to the editor. Surprisingly, I did not receive much flack from the public. Perhaps those who opposed my point of view simply wrote me off as misguided. On the other hand, meeting people in the grocery store or on the street who thanked me for what I had written affirmed me in my conviction to speak out on behalf of peace.

Calling people to right relationship with God and each other is dangerous. Remember what happened to the prophets and to Jesus. Yet, what is the Christian life worth if one does not hold onto the integrity of the Gospel? Standing up for justice takes many forms, but it will always demand a fundamental deep trust in God. From that source, whatever one chooses to do moves to a different level where the presence of God is a steadying hand of courage.

How does Gospel-centered justice express itself in your life today?

Connecting the Charism

Justice

"Hold fast to patience with a silent mind when in this obedience [you are met] with difficulties and contradictions and even any kind of injustice, enduring all without growing weary or running away." Rule of St. Benedict 7:35

Justice is the flip side of charity. Charity responds to needs while justice works to eliminate the causes of those needs. A well-known proverb demonstrates this: Give a poor person a fish, and that person's hunger is sated. Teach the person how to fish, and he or she no longer needs to be hungry. Throughout the Hebrew Scriptures, Yahweh exhorts the people to care for widows and orphans and strangers in the land. Yahweh says it's the right thing to do because the Hebrew people themselves were once strangers in a foreign land. Empathy and compassion promote works of charity and justice.

Justice finds its roots in the Incarnation. All human beings have dignity because the Son of God became a human being. Therefore, whenever social, economic, ethnic, or religious structures threaten or deny the dignity of persons, we as disciples of Jesus Christ are called to intervene. For living our baptism includes the responsibility of building a just society. That's how I got involved in peace and justice work. The lives of my sisters and brothers in Christ were being threatened by some of the products designed for warfare that Honeywell was manufacturing. The lives lost forever in the wars being waged around the globe and people thrown into chaos as refugees, displaced persons, those on hit lists or wrongly imprisoned, those (mostly women and girls) ravaged by the "winning" side or sold into prostitution—all this and more cried out, and I felt compelled to respond even though I wondered what I could do in the face of such huge issues.

In one of his homilies Archbishop Oscar Romero revealed an answer:

> *We cannot do everything, and there is a sense of liberation in realizing that. This enables us to do something, and to do it very well. It may be*

incomplete, but it is a beginning, a step along the way and an opportunity for the Lord's grace to enter and to do the rest."[5]

In the short run, standing on the street corner with signs calling for peace probably did not accomplish much. Nonetheless, it was a small step to greater awareness for all who saw us there week after week. They learned that not everybody was in favor of the buildup or invasion of Iraq. From reading our letters in the local paper, they learned why we insisted that there had to be another way. We were about changing the hearts and minds of our fellow townsmen and women. In the process of bearing witness to peace, my heart and mind were changed in significant ways:

- I grieved with the families on both sides who had lost a soldier or family member(s) in the fighting.
- My heart ached for those who were forced to leave their homes and possessions to seek refuge in neighboring countries where often they were not welcome.
- I grew angry over the poisoning of the Earth from spent uranium warheads on the bombs our country was dropping and the many Iraqi children and adults who would become sick and die because of them.
- I worried over fanaticism when the letter of the law supersedes the spirit of the law, whether in the Middle East or in this country, in politics and in religion.
- I learned the necessity and urgency of working for justice, of advocating for those who could not speak for themselves, and of joining with others in campaigns to keep people informed about the issues and what they mean in light of Catholic Social Teaching.
- I valued the people committed to the same goals who supported and encouraged my actions for peace.
- I recognized that the Franciscan tradition that I live as an Associate of the Franciscan Sisters of Little Falls grounds my peace and justice work with vision, conviction, and courage.

[5] *The Prayer of Oscar Romero.*

Benedictine Sister Joan Chittister, renowned speaker and prolific author, is a marvelous contemporary model of someone with a tireless and undaunted commitment to justice. She speaks out fearlessly on the issues of our day, examining them in the penetrating light of the Gospel. She wrote in *Called to Question:*

> *"The truth is, I think, that what we don't name we enable. We become blind to the evils in which we live and breathe and call our culture. We take the unacceptable as natural. We take injustice for granted. We call sin normal. But if and when we begin to call evil, evil . . . then we ourselves begin to confront the problem."*[6]

"If and when we begin to call evil, evil . . ." describes the role of the prophet. Scripture reveals to us that God raised up prophets—the greatest of them Jesus—to call the people back to fidelity to the covenant God had made with them. "This is what Yahweh asks of you," wrote the prophet Micah, "Only this, to act justly, to love tenderly and to walk humbly with your God" (Mic 6:8). Today God continues to raise up prophets with the same message: To remain faithful to the covenant God makes with us through our baptism.

How do you overcome the fear of acting on your faith to stand up and speak out against the injustice that you witness?

[6] Chittister, Joan. *Called to Question: A Spiritual Memoir*. Kansas City: Sheed & Ward, 2009. Print.

STEWARDSHIP

The Story

"I would like you to move from the Office of Youth and Young Adult Ministries to a teaching position at the Ministry Formation Institute," the new bishop was saying to me. "I have asked several people, including both vicars general, who would be a great teacher, and all have put forth your name." I had been the Diocesan Director of Youth and Young Adult Ministries for eight years and looked forward to continuing in this role under the new bishop. The bishop's offer came as a shock because it would be a demotion.

My two ministerial loves have been youth ministry and teaching theology. In 1996 I left teaching theology at a high school to become Diocesan Director of Youth and Young Adult Ministries. By 2003, the administrative tasks and conflicts of the position began to weigh heavily. Although I loved youth and young adult ministries, it became apparent that the work of administration was not my gift. I could do it, but it was not life giving.

As I struggled with the challenges in my professional role, personal events in my life intensified the pressure. My father, from whom I had been estranged for most of my adult life, passed away in the fall of 2000 less than a month after I took the initiative to reconnect with him after twenty years. In the grief that followed, a family member revealed that a priest who had been a youth minister when we were growing up had abused him. This personalized the trauma of the sexual abuse scandal just as the diocese was beginning to face its impact.

In the summer of 2003, the local county attorney indicted six active or former priests on sexual abuse charges. One of these indictments was against the person who abused my family member. In the days following the public announcement of the indictments, our bishop would strike and kill a pedestrian and then fail to stop. The cumulative effects of the abuse crisis and his widely publicized arrest for the accident led to his resignation. On the day of the bishop's resignation, the apostolic administrator offered these words to the chancery staff, "Put your faith in God, not in me, or any other human person. We will always disappoint. God will never disappoint."

In September of that year, my gift as a teacher was put to the test. Diocesan officials approached me to research, write, and implement a safe environment training program. In the next five months my world centered on implementing the program. Night after night I was teaching and facilitating. Because the program critically evaluated some practices that had become standard in youth ministry programs, audiences were often hostile. People said that the new policies and procedures advanced by the program were ruining the ability for individuals to minister effectively with teens. My efforts to eliminate the possibilities of abuse happening in the church were misconstrued as killing youth ministry, hindering effectiveness, and establishing structures that prevented "good relational ministry."

My world began to spin. I was angry and confused, working in a structure that created an abusive culture from which my own family was not immune. I perceived others' dislike of what I did as criticism of me. In those months, my anger and frustration grew as my passion to do something good soured. I wanted to make things right for my family member who had been abused, for other victims, and for my dad. At the same time, the anger and resentment boiling just under the surface made me a very passionate presenter, and I believed that I was changing things. This belief was confirmed in November when the diocese was audited for compliance to the Dallas Charter and given a commendation. Even this commendation from the USCCB did not reduce my inner turmoil.

No one could see the pain I was experiencing. I was working more than I had ever worked in my life. Each day my internal conflict grew, and I don't like conflict. I like to escape and during this time, I found it through compulsive gambling binges. Before I knew it, I had spent days and a lot of money, escaping in the mornings and working for safe environments in the evenings. The turmoil didn't ease, but the compulsion provided a world where I didn't have to deal with feelings that I was inferior in administration, destroying youth ministry, or betraying family members because I worked for the church. The anger and frustration at myself, at the church and at God spun in me like a hurricane gathering steam. How could I put my faith in God in the midst of so much pain? Now, more than ever was the time for self-reliance!

I quickly learned that self-reliance was not an option. The love and honesty of friends and family helped me to realize that I was moving on a path of destruction and into a valley of death. I found a good 12-step group and began my abstinence. In January I was asked to drop the work on the safe environments program and re-focus on youth and young adult ministries. Immediately thereafter, the safe environment training began to be changed. I was resentful; the program had been commended by the USCCB, so why would it need to be changed? How could attitudes toward behaviors that had led to this mess in the first place be softened? The community had called me forth to do this work, but what I accomplished was changing. Was it all for naught?

On top of all this, the new bishop was now asking me to leave youth and young adult ministry altogether and enter a new role teaching adults. I hadn't done anything wrong. I had served youth and young adult ministries faithfully, and when the diocese needed me, I worked the hardest I had ever worked. The program that I had written earned the diocese a commendation. My sense of duty, responsibility, comfort and pride was telling me to stay in youth ministry.

I had become so wrapped up in myself that I couldn't recognize my giftedness actually being stewarded. I had forgotten that the work I was doing was a gift in service of Christ and the church and instead made it about me. While I initially resisted the move into adult education, the recognition of my gifts by the community led me to the safe environment work, and now the new bishop was inviting me to share those gifts to deepen people's understanding of the church's theology as they prepared for ministry. What I was experiencing was not rejection of my past work but a calling forth and stewarding of gifts that would benefit others. It is a lesson that has deeply affected how I attend to stewarding gifts with those with whom and among I minister.

In what ways does your own experience with stewardship connect with this story?

How does this story shape your vocational call?

What does hearing this story with "the ear of the heart" illuminate in you as you explore the practice of ministry?

Valley of the Dry Bones
Ezekiel 37:1-14

The hand of the LORD came upon me, and he brought me out by the spirit of the LORD and set me down in the middle of a valley; it was full of bones. He led me all round them; there were very many lying in the valley, and they were very dry. He said to me, "Mortal, can these bones live?" I answered, "O Lord GOD, you know." Then he said to me, "Prophesy to these bones, and say to them: O dry bones, hear the word of the LORD. Thus says the Lord GOD to these bones: I will cause breath to enter you, and you shall live. I will lay sinews on you, and will cause flesh to come upon you, and cover you with skin, and put breath in you, and you shall live; and you shall know that I am the LORD."

So I prophesied as I had been commanded; and as I prophesied, suddenly there was a noise, a rattling, and the bones came together, bone to its bone. I looked, and there were sinews on them, and flesh had come upon them, and skin had covered them; but there was no breath in them. Then he said to me, "Prophesy to the breath, prophesy, mortal, and say to the breath: Thus says the Lord GOD: Come from the four winds, O breath, and breathe upon these slain, that they may live." I prophesied as he commanded me, and the breath came into them, and they lived, and stood on their feet, a vast multitude.

Then he said to me, "Mortal, these bones are the whole house of Israel. They say, 'Our bones are dried up, and our hope is lost; we are cut off completely.' Therefore prophesy, and say to them, Thus says the Lord GOD: I am going to open your graves, and bring you up from your graves, O my people; and I will bring you back to the land of Israel. And you shall know that I am the LORD, when I open your graves, and bring you up from your graves, O my people. I will put my spirit within you, and you shall live, and I will place you on your own soil; then you shall know that I, the LORD, have spoken and will act," says the LORD.

Valley of the Dry Bones, Donald Jackson, 2005, *The Saint John's Bible*, Hill Museum & Manuscript Library, Order of Saint Benedict, Collegeville, Minnesota, USA.

devour people and no longer bereave your nation
of children, says the Lord GOD; [15] and no longer will
I let you hear the insults of the nations, no longer
shall you bear the disgrace of the peoples; and no
longer shall you cause your nation to stumble, says
16 the Lord GOD. The word of the LORD came to me:
[17] Mortal, when the house of Israel lived on their
own soil, they defiled it with their ways and their
deeds; their conduct in my sight was like the un
cleanness of a woman in her menstrual period. [18] So
I poured out my wrath upon them for the blood that
they had shed upon the land, and for the idols with
which they had defiled it. [19] I scattered them among
the nations, and they were dispersed through the
countries; in accordance with their conduct & their
deeds I judged them. [20] But when they came to the
nations, wherever they came, they profaned my holy
name, in that it was said of them, "These are the peo
ple of the LORD, and yet they had to go out of his
land." [21] But I had concern for my holy name, which
the house of Israel had profaned among the nations
22 to which they came. Therefore say to the house
of Israel, Thus says the Lord GOD: It is not for your
sake, O house of Israel, that I am about to act, but
for the sake of my holy name, which you have pro
faned among the nations to which you came. [23] I will
sanctify my great name, which has been profaned
among the nations, and which you have profaned
among them; and the nations shall know that I am
the LORD, says the Lord GOD, when through you I
display my holiness before their eyes. [24] I will take
you from the nations, and gather you from all the
countries, and bring you into your own land. [25] I will
sprinkle clean water upon you, and you shall be clean
from all your uncleannesses, and from all your idols
I will cleanse you. [26] A new heart I will give you, and
a new spirit I will put within you; and I will remove
from your body the heart of stone and give you a
heart of flesh. [27] I will put my spirit within you, and
make you follow my statutes and be careful to ob
serve my ordinances. [28] Then you shall live in the land
that I gave to your ancestors; and you shall be my
people, and I will be your God. [29] I will save you from
all your uncleannesses, and I will summon the grain
and make it abundant and lay no famine upon you.
[30] I will make the fruit of the tree and the produce
of the field abundant, so that you may never again
suffer the disgrace of famine among the nations.
[31] Then you shall remember your evil ways, and your
dealings that were not good; and you shall loathe
yourselves for your iniquities and your abominable
deeds. [32] It is not for your sake that I will act, says
the Lord GOD; let that be known to you. Be ashamed
33 & dismayed for your ways, O house of Israel. Thus
says the Lord GOD: On the day that I cleanse you from
all your iniquities, I will cause the towns to be in
habited, and the waste places shall be rebuilt. [34] The
land that was desolate shall be tilled, instead of be
ing the desolation that it was in the sight of all who
passed by. [35] And they will say, "This land that was
desolate has become like the garden of Eden; and
the waste and desolate and ruined towns are now
inhabited and fortified." [36] Then the nations that are
left all around you shall know that I, the LORD, have
rebuilt the ruined places, and replanted that which
was desolate; I, the LORD, have spoken, and I will
37 do it. Thus says the Lord GOD: I will also let the
house of Israel ask me to do this for them: to increase
their population like a flock. [38] Like the flock for sac
rifices, like the flock at Jerusalem during her ap
pointed festivals, so shall the ruined towns be filled
with flocks of people. Then they shall know that I
am the LORD.

37

The hand of the LORD came upon me, and he brought
me out by the spirit of the LORD and set me down
in the middle of a valley; it was full of bones. 2 He
led me all around them; there were very many lying
in the valley, and they were very dry. 3 He said to me,
"Mortal, can these bones live?" I answered, "O Lord
GOD, you know." 4 Then he said to me, "Prophesy to
these bones, and say to them: O dry bones, hear the
word of the LORD. 5 Thus says the Lord GOD to these
bones: I will cause breath[p] to enter you, and you shall
live. 6 I will lay sinews on you, and will cause flesh
to come upon you, and cover you with skin, and put
breath[q] in you, and you shall live; and you shall know
7 that I am the LORD." So I prophesied as I had been
commanded; and as I prophesied, suddenly there
was a noise, a rattling, and the bones came together,
bone to its bone. 8 I looked, and there were sinews on
them, and flesh had come upon them, and skin
had covered them; but there was no breath in them.
9 Then he said to me, "Prophesy to the breath,[r] proph-
esy, mortal, and say to the breath:[s] Thus says the
Lord GOD: Come from the four winds, O breath, and
breathe upon these slain, that they may live." 10 I
prophesied as he commanded me, and the breath
came into them, and they lived, and stood on their
11 feet, a vast multitude. Then he said to me, "Mortal,
these bones are the whole house of Israel. They say,
'Our bones are dried up, and our hope is lost; we are
cut off completely.' 12 Therefore prophesy, and say
to them, Thus says the Lord GOD: I am going to open
your graves, and bring you up from your graves, O my
people; and I will bring you back to the land of Is-
rael. 13 And you shall know that I am the LORD, when I
open your graves, and bring you up from your graves,
O my people. 14 I will put my spirit within you, and
you shall live, and I will place you on your own soil;
then you shall know that I, the LORD, have spoken
and will act, says the LORD."

15 The word of the LORD came to me: 16 Mortal, take
a stick and write on it, "For Judah, and the Israelites
associated with it"; then take another stick & write
on it, "For Joseph (the stick of Ephraim) and all the
house of Israel associated with it"; 17 and join them
together into one stick, so that they may become
one in your hand. 18 And when your people say to
you, "Will you not show us what you mean by these?"
19 say to them, Thus says the Lord GOD: I am about
to take the stick of Joseph (which is in the hand of
Ephraim) and the tribes of Israel associated with it;
and I will put the stick of Judah upon it,[t] and make
them one stick, in order that they may be one in my
hand. 20 When the sticks on which you write are in
your hand before their eyes, 21 then say to them, Thus
says the Lord GOD: I will take the people of Israel
from the nations among which they have gone, and
will gather them from every quarter, and bring them
to their own land. 22 I will make them one nation in
the land, on the mountains of Israel; and one king
shall be king over them all. Never again shall they
be two nations, and never again shall they be divided
into two kingdoms. 23 They shall never again defile
themselves with their idols & their detestable things,
or with any of their transgressions. I will save them
from all the apostasies into which they have fallen,[u]
and will cleanse them. Then they shall be my people,
24 and I will be their God. My servant David shall
be king over them; and they shall all have one shep-
herd. They shall follow my ordinances and be careful
to observe my statutes. 25 They shall live in the land
that I gave to my servant Jacob, in which your ances-
tors lived; they and their children & their children's

o Heb flesh of holy things
p,q Or spirit
r,s Or wind or spirit
t Heb I will put them upon it
u Another reading is from all the settlements in which they have sinned

Reflection on the Illuminated Word

Ezekiel is placed in the role of the ultimate steward as he must prophesy to the 'dry bones' who were the people Israel. This is a concept of stewardship that is often overlooked and not brought forth. Ezekiel is not called to be the steward of the land or the goods of the earth. Instead, he is called by God to become a steward of persons, called to prophesy in the midst of a community's and an individual's dryness, and by doing so, bring them to life. There are three realities presented in this passage. The first is the dry bones. The second is the role of Ezekiel as a prophet. The third is God's action with the people through Ezekiel's vision.

Seeing the dry bones is distressing. In the illumination, one sees the piles of bones, skulls and glasses reminding us of the Holocaust and other attempts at genocide in our time. Also visible are windows and shattered panes of glass, reminiscent of the aftermath of the Twin Towers at Ground Zero following 9/11. In the foreground one can see the forms of vehicles, abandoned and thrown away. The text and image call us to ask ourselves how we have entered a Valley of Dry Bones.

As ministers, we often become so obsessed with our performance and with ourselves that we manipulate to get the results that we desire, failing to listen to the desires of God. We consume to our heart's content and buy into the myths that the one who has more possessions or more success will somehow win the rat race. It is a myth that eats at the heart of our human being and leads us deeply into the valley of dryness. Just as the Israelites understood their exile to be rooted in an idolatry that led them away from their covenantal relationships, so we in the twenty-first century must confront the idols of materialism, success and the temptation to manipulate that lead us into valleys of dry bones.

Can we allow ourselves to be stewarded beyond this?

As Ezekiel beholds the vision of the Valley of Dry Bones, God asks him, "Mortal, can these bones live?" (Ezek 37:3). Ezekiel, appearing a bit frustrated replies, "O Lord God, you know." The dialogue evokes a scene of the master teacher asking a question of a tired and wary student who just wants to know the answer. As the master teacher begins to respond, an exciting and dynamic reality unfolds. The journey in ministry is often like this. We scream at God as we stand in the midst of the dry bones, often exhausted and frustrated because God is seemingly asking us to engage the impossible task of stewarding dry bones to life. We think we must do this ourselves, or we stand in the dusty valley and respond as Ezekiel, "O Lord God, you know?"

The figures rising from the cloud of dust and waste appear to be struggling and straining to come to life. Ministers who live in the valley of dryness often become comfortable. In our comfort, it is easier to stay in the valley, continuing to be a dried skeleton on the desert floor. We remain rattling bones and sinews, resisting the breath of God as we hold on to the belief that we can give the dry bones we encounter a new sense of life. We think and believe that we are doing God's work, often ignoring the wind that blows and calls us, as ministers, to life.

Finally, our focus must shift to the action of God. In the illumination everything is moving upward toward the glory of God. God's glory appears to be pulling the human figures from the bones as they are brought rattling, connecting and gasping, from the piles. God acts as steward to them, calling them into life. Ezekiel's proclamation mediates the action, and the breath of God affects it. The Spirit enters them, and they live.

Where do you find yourself in this illumination? How does that place impact your call to ministry?

Connecting the Charism

Stewardship

"If there are artisans in the monastery, they are to practice their craft with all humility . . . so that in all things God may be glorified." The Rule of St. Benedict 57

In the first year of my work for the Ministry Formation Institute, I struggled. Yet, no matter how tired or frustrated I was before each class, I would leave having watched and experienced an exciting and dynamic reality unfold, just as it had for Ezekiel in the Valle of Dry Bones. I began to realize that this work was energizing me. Through the work that I was doing, God was breathing life back into me. The bishop's practice of stewardship, a stewardship that centered on bringing forth the giftedness of the individual, opened me to God's breath being breathed into me. I was living again, practicing my craft of teaching, and God was being glorified through it.

We are responsible for the stewardship of creation, of possessions, of finances, of health care, and other aspects of life. Yet, stewardship makes no sense whatsoever if all we are doing in the practice of the charism is stewarding things. The call to stewardship is first and foremost a call to steward people. This call rests in the belief that each person is a gift and demands an encounter with other persons. Likewise, they deserve a discernment of his or her practical gifts, and encouragement to place those gifts in the service of Christ and the human community.

In a book titled, *Now Discover Your Strengths* (Buckingham and Clifton. The Gallup Organization. 2001), the authors point out that most of us spend our lives, personally and professionally, developing and improving our weaknesses rather than our strengths. They offer a different model, rooted in hefty research of effective managers. Those who bring forth the strengths of the people with whom they work will find themselves with happier and more deeply fulfilled employees.

Many of us who share in the work of ministry are not well stewarded. We buy into the comfort of the routine, the fear of what is different, the anger that the Church and God have hurt us, or the idea that our gifts are not worthy contributions to the church. We retain our roles out of a sense of duty and a fear of the unknown rather than seeking to minister from the wonder and excitement within us. We become piles of dry bones in catechetical sessions, choir practices and on altars as we wait for some Ezekiel to come into our lives and prophesy while we are saying, "Our bones are dried up, and our hope is lost; we are cut off completely" (Ezek 37:11b).

The essence of stewardship and the task for those called to be stewards in the work of ministry is two-fold. First, we must discern how well the work in which we are engaged is a stewardship of our person and the gifts that we have been given. Second, we must facilitate the gifts and strengths of those with whom we work. Rooted in the depth of dignity that acknowledges the being (the very existence of the person) and function (the things that the person does well) of self and other as gift, the next logical step is to offer this giftedness to be made holy. Understood in this manner, stewardship is ultimately Eucharistic. The gift of each individual—their being and their function offered in union with the gift of Christ—is placed on the altar to be made holy and offered in the service of God and the human community.

This action helps us to realize that we are not the source of our lives or the source of our own giftedness, and it empowers us to recall God's breath within. When offering and utilizing my giftedness for the sake of self, my end was clear: I walked and lived in the Valley of Dry Bones. When I allowed myself to be stewarded to a fuller and deeper use and realization of these gifts and ultimately myself, I was enlivened. To become enlivened through this sense of stewardship will empower us to proclaim, paraphrasing St. Irenaeus, *the glory of God is the human being fully alive!*[7]

[7] *St. Irenaeus of Lyons: Against the Heresies Book 1v (Ancient Christian Writers).* Westminster: Newman Press, 1991. Print.

What gifts do you have that others are unaware of? How would the empowerment of these gifts impact the community in which you live and worship?

CONVERSATIO

The Story

No one enters a monastery hoping they will become the vocation director. The prioress or abbot entrusts this ministry to those who have "fallen in love" with the monastic way of life and have the potential to share its goodness with others discerning a vocation. Without a doubt it is the most challenging, inspiring ministry I have ever done. The past six years, admittedly both gift and cross, have led me deeper into the graced reality of monastic life and made me more aware of God's movement in the lives of seekers. That is not to say that this ministry has been easy.

I soon discovered that being the Director of Vocation Ministry meant leaving the confines of the monastery to raise awareness of our very existence and hopefully to draw the curious faithful to the monastery for a taste of our life. There was no "net" to cast out—no magic slogan. I just did my best to tell our Benedictine story and answer many really good questions. If a relationship was begun, I was called to simply listen "with the ear of [my] heart," to companion each candidate over a period of months—sometimes years—to a place of relative certainty, and to nurture the seed of God's call over time until it was ready for the harvest.[8] I've seen at least eleven women through a sea of paperwork and a battery of psychological tests that might make even Jesus a bit nervous. I've asked them to write their life stories and received them with reverence—each a gospel in miniature replete with Good Fridays, Holy Saturdays and resurrections. All the while

[8] Benedict, and Timothy Fry. "Prologue 1." *RB 1980: The Rule of St. Benedict in English*. Collegeville, Minn.: Liturgical Press, 1982.

all members of the community prayed that their lives would be God's plan for each of them.

When a candidate comes, we see a future graced by their presence in the monastery. We see the manifold gifts recognized and untapped. In each woman, we see our way of life continuing by the deliberate grace of God. Each time a woman knocked on the chapel door and entered the monastery, I felt a deep joy that made the most arduous efforts seem small. Determined from my first day on the job to place the burden of this ministry squarely in God's hands, I told my happy sisters—eager to affirm my gifts and skills—that our newest member was God's work. To God be the glory. This strategy held me in good stead—*until* a woman left our monastery.

When a woman decides to leave the monastery, it is like a death. As suitcases are packed and placed in the hallway, we walk softly past her doorway, confident that God is at work but grieving a love that is lost to us—a future we will never share. "*Their passing away [is] thought an affliction; their going forth from us, utter destruction*" (Wis 3:2-3). The first time it happened after I became vocation director, I lost my footing completely. I couldn't make sense of it. What had I done wrong? What didn't I see in all her paperwork? What did we miss in the psychological tests? How could I go forward as vocation director if my gut instinct was faulty? All that I believed about my own gifts for the ministry now seemed tenuous.

Kristen was special. Okay, she was special to me. There was some "little sister" thing going on there. I saw something familiar in her. I had hopes and dreams for Kristen and even though her trajectory had some twists and turns, I really believed that she had a monastic heart. Admittedly, I lost clarity and objectivity early on. But, trusting in our process and the many tests along the way, I thought in the end that she was meant to be a Benedictine sister. I was wrong. We were wrong. I cried the day she left and for several days thereafter. It was a loss for the community and undeniably a loss for me.

No matter how many women have entered the monastery under my guidance, it was the one who left who wound up teaching me the most about God's grace. In the midst of my grief and suffering came wisdom. It was so easy to give God the credit when good things were happening (after all, God and I were working together). It was much harder not to blame myself when things went "wrong." I forgot that God is always God—in our joy and in our suffering. God directs the vocational journey—when a person comes and when a person decides to leave

I have come to rest more comfortably in the mystery of God's call. Seekers will continue to come. Some will stay. Some will leave. I believe that their coming has meaning even if they do not stay with us. The learning is mutual in this enterprise. The sisters and the seeker are on the road together.

The mystery of God's call, however, extends beyond the journey of one religious community. I have come to clearer insight about the tension between personal definitions of success and failure and how they can deceive one about the way God works in our lives. Success and failure are part of the rhythm of life well-lived. If we are reflective ministers, they can teach us about patience, courage and fidelity even in the face of what we might perceive as defeat.

In what ways does your own experience in finding the heart of God connect with this story?

How does this story shape your vocational call?

What does hearing this story with "the ear of the heart" illuminate in you as you explore the practice of ministry?

Job Frontispiece
Job 2:3-10

The LORD said to Satan, "Have you considered my servant Job? There is no one like him on the earth, a blameless and upright man who fears God and turns away from evil. He still persists in his integrity, although you incited me against him, to destroy him for no reason." Then Satan answered the LORD, "Skin for skin! All that people have they will give to save their lives. But stretch out your hand now and touch his bone and his flesh, and he will curse you to your face." The LORD said to Satan, "Very well, he is in your power; only spare his life."

So Satan went out from the presence of the LORD, and inflicted loathsome sores on Job from the sole of his foot to the crown of his head. Job took a potsherd with which to scrape himself, and sat among the ashes.

Then his wife said to him, "Do you still persist in your integrity? Curse God, and die." But he said to her, "You speak as any foolish woman would speak. Shall we receive the good at the hand of God, and not receive the bad?" In all this Job did not sin with his lips.

Job Frontispiece, Donald Jackson, 2006, *The Saint John's Bible*, Hill Museum & Manuscript Library, Order of Saint Benedict, Collegeville, Minnesota, USA.

Lectio • Meditatio • Visio • Oratio • Contemplatio • Conversatio

Reflection on the Illuminated Word

Poor Job! Most of us haven't even read the full story, but we know that Job loses everything—his home, his family, his livelihood—all as part of some cosmic game show in which God allows Satan to give it his best shot. Job never cries "uncle." He never abandons the God of his ancestors. Job does, however, have a few questions for the Almighty—questions that seem to me quite understandable given the horrors of his test. It is in the midst of those questions that Job learns the most important lesson of all: God is mystery even as God is fully present.

The illumination from the Book of Job offers us an unsentimental view of the inner chaos of being human. Joy and suffering are side by side—inseparable partners in the dance of life. Suffering, seen on the right, is dark and ugly—a vortex of passion and pain. Joy, on the left, is beauty in motion—a fireworks display of hope and possibility. What is most intriguing about this piece is the artist's refusal to place one above the other. We cannot choose joy alone. Life hurts; there is pain and sorrow and suffering. Each has its place in every story, and, like Job, we may wonder, "Why?" Job's story teaches us a valuable lesson—without the boils. Contradictions of life are part of the mystery of God. We can't answer or resolve all the questions the world poses. It is only in recognizing that our joys and sorrows are part of our story and our search for God that we can let go of the questions which keep us from living in the present and entrust our lives to the One who was there when the oceans were made. At the very beginning of his trials, Job knew this very truth. *"Shall we receive the good at the hand of God, and not receive the bad?"* If God is God, then we have nothing to fear.

As you reflect on the vortex of pain personally, communally and for the world, what are your "Why?" questions? How are you able to reconcile the contradictions of life as a part of the mystery of God?

Connecting the Charism

Conversatio

"Receive me, O Lord, according to Your word, and I shall live: and let me not be confounded in my hope" (Ps 118[119]:116). The Rule of St. Benedict 58

In RB 58 Saint Benedict spells out the procedure for receiving new members into the monastery, and in so doing he gives us the heart of the monastic enterprise. The newcomer is to promise obedience, stability and *conversatio*—currently translated as "Fidelity to the monastic way of life." *Conversatio* is not just for monks and nuns, however. It is integral to the life of every Christian. Esther de Waal, an Episcopalian Oblate of Saint Benedict and prolific writer on Benedictine spirituality believes that *conversatio* is "Recognition of God's unpredictability, which confronts our own love of coziness or safety . . . It means a constant letting go."

As Director of Vocation Ministry, I have learned the hard way to stand in the middle. I walk with women who feel called to our life, but I am keenly aware that we do not walk alone. God is beside her and beside me in the middle of the unknowing we call "discernment." Sometimes it is in the biggest disappointments that God shows me something new—teaches me to trust that there will be blessing. The promise I made years ago is ever-present to me in this ministry. Each woman is on her journey to God. I cannot take a specific outcome as the last word. We—she and I—are unfinished. *Conversatio* calls me to let go of what happens next and trust that God is doing something. The unexpected twists and turns in each life are really grist for the mill. If we can embrace what is instead of longing for what cannot be, we will be certain to meet God in the middle.

It isn't easy. Often, it comes with not a little suffering. But *conversatio* is the gift of still-becoming. It is God's promise of presence as we make the next movement into a grace-filled future. *Conversatio* is, very simply, the Christian path to the heart of God.

As you make your way to the heart of God—where do you stumble, where do you find resolution and where do you find joy?

CONTRIBUTORS

Mark Barder (Hospitality) is the director of the permanent diaconate and planning consultant for the Diocese of St. Cloud, Minnesota.

Alan Wielinski (Community) is pastor of St. Peter Parish and St. Paul Parish in St. Cloud, Minnesota.

Mary Martin (Listening) is a chaplain at the University of Minnesota Medical Center and a spiritual director at the Benedictine Center of St. Paul's Monastery in St. Paul, Minnesota.

Diana McCarney (Reverence for All People) is principal of St. Phillip's Catholic School, Litchfield, Minnesota.

Judy Virnig (Justice) coordinates the Office for Franciscan Associates in Little Falls, Minnesota.

Larry Fraher (Stewardship) is the director of catechetical ministries at the Community of the Blessed Sacrament in Scottsdale, Arizona.

Vicki Ix, OSB (Conversatio) is vocation director and a member of the Benedictine Community in Bristow, Virginia.

Victor Klimoski (Editor) is director of lifelong learning for the School of Theology•Seminary, Saint John's University, Collegeville, Minnesota.

Barbara Sutton (Editor) is associate dean for formation and outreach for the School of Theology•Seminary, Saint John's University, Collegeville, Minnesota.